Sustainable Country Living

A guide to living through troubled times.

Donn Leiske, M.Ed. CTE

Sustainable Country Living

Volume 1 of the "Preparing for the Time of Trouble" Series

Cover Design: Donn Leiske

Copyright 2024 by Donn Leiske

Produced by Prepare Publications

Date of Original Publication: January 2024

Date of Latest Publication: November 2024

Contents

Introduction

The world is changing, and much of it, is not for the better. On a global scale, we are seeing in the news, an ever-increasing frequency of natural disasters, as often characterized by news commentators as "apocalyptic" or of "biblical proportions". These seemingly unprecedented natural disasters are frequently described as the worst of its kind in modern history. These can be seen in a steady increase in intensity and frequency of droughts resulting in wildfires and torrential rain episodes causing mass flooding. Then there are massive wind events from tornados, cyclones, hurricanes, and typhoons. All of these kinds of natural disasters often result in not just property damage but great loss of human lives. The outcomes are devastating enough that it can take many generations to recoup and rebuild.

The urban centers are becoming more and more dangerous with a steady increase of homeless tent cities, littered with discarded drug paraphernalia of junkies. Those living, of necessity, in these homeless encampments are themselves in an ever-dangerous environment, gripping on to every scrap of earthly possession, housed in stolen shopping carts, in an effort to not have these last vestiges of worldly belongings being stolen by others, leaving them even more destitute.

The political policies of the defunding of police have hand-tied those who remain in law enforcement. These directives keep police from being able to stop extreme violence resulting in paralyzing business establishments due to the increased instances of "smash and grab" robberies of businesses in the large cities. This has caused many respected drug stores and retail businesses to close in the cities, leaving behind abandoned retail spaces, waiting for further damage and defacing with graffiti.

So, what should a person do to get out of the dangers and the potential of impending doom of the large urban centers? The answer is to get out of harm's way by embracing the country living lifestyle and enjoying a productive, fulfilling, and peaceful life in nature!

Chapter 1: Urban Dangers

There was a time in America when most families lived in the country. Before the Industrial Revolution, family farms were prevalent and for the most part, were self-sustaining. Often these early home farms were without dependence on electricity. Lighting was by kerosene lamps and water from the well was powered by a windmill. These homesteads raised their own produce, meats, and dairy products. Because the daily responsibilities were many and varied, families were usually large.

Historic Migration to the Cities

The American Industrial Revolution in the late 1700s provided employment opportunities for many on the family farms to find a more financially improved life off the farm. In most cases, this career change resulted in moving off the family farm and into the cities of industry. Over the years the cities quickly grew, and the family farm model diminished. Future centuries saw a steady change in how farming was done, with ever-increasing dependence on larger and more sophisticated equipment to mechanize the farm processes. This resulted in a steady increase in the size of the farms, with many eventually becoming corporate farms.

Vanishing Family Farms

Today the family farm has all but vanished, and young people wishing to make a living owning a farm, find themselves literally priced out of the market unless they are fortunate enough to inherit the land and the farm operation. This phenomenon has made moving to the country more and more difficult as time progresses. During this evolution of American lifestyles, people found living in the city appealing, offering more casual time and seemingly endless opportunities for entertainment, and eating out. The appeal of living in the country has diminished to the point that now few even wish to live in the country.

Bread Line During the Great Depression image source:
Library of Congress

Urban Dangers During the Great Depression

With the boom of American cities came money and lives of leisure. Then came the Great Depression. We have all seen images of "work wanted" signs being held up by able-bodied men and pictures of soup lines. There are pictures of people desperate for a handout of food and sleeping on the sidewalks and train stations with only a newspaper for a bed. These sad situations that we have seen portrayed, have one thing in common...location. This period of nationwide hardship was particularly evident in the cities.

The Country Way

By contrast, those fortunate enough to still live on a family farm saw very little impact during the Great Depression. Dr. Lloyd Eighme, in his book "The Country Way", explains how his parent's family of five weathered the Great Depression on a small two-acre family farm. His book not only describes living off their gardens and a cow for milk, but the book includes a drawing of the farm, mapping out what was grown and where, and describes the rotation of crops. As a young person, he witnessed his parents live through this period of hard times because they did not live in a city, but on a self-sustaining family farm, even though it was only two acres (Eighme, 1976).

The Country Way Book Cover used with permission from
Mary Margaret Eighme

Urban Dangers in the Modern City

Many of the large, progressive cities of today have ever-increasing elements of danger. These have enacted policies of defunding the police and putting in place new laws with weakened penalties for previously illegal activities such as decriminalizing drug possession by demoting that infraction to a simple misdemeanor. As a result, we have seen a major increase in crime in the cities, including the "smash and grab" robberies, where large groups of thugs storm a jewelry store or pharmacy and steal an armful of inventory. Many large stores now instruct their employees to do nothing to stop these large-scale shoplifting operations. We now see big box home improvement stores having to lock up everything from power tools to electrical wires, to protect their inventory. Even stores like Walmart and Target must lock up electronic items such as computers or anything small enough to hide in shoplifter's pockets. Many large retail chains have closed their downtown places of business because it is now too dangerous for employees and the ever-increasing loss of profitability from out-of-control shoplifting.

Marked Contrast

Driving through large cities now, one sees a marked contrast between how things were 10 or 20 years ago to what is presently seen: empty retail spaces and corporate buildings; large tent city encampments; littered garbage; and miles of graffiti along the streets and highways. One large city was visited by a contingent of representatives scouting where to hold the next large, national convention. After being attacked on the street in broad daylight, the committee decided to find a different location, even though the organization had historically used that same city each year. On an almost daily basis, we hear on the news about some mass shootings in the cities with shocking numbers of innocent people injured or killed. Just like the example of the Great Depression, once again there seems to be one common denominator to these problems...location. The dangers in urban centers are on a steady rise.

The Pressure to Stay in the Cities

Despite these obvious negative elements related to living in the cities, there is an increasing pressure to encourage people to move into or stay in the cities. One such approach is called "New Urbanist Neighborhoods". According to a book published by the US Green Building Council, "Most of the dwellings are within a five-minute walk to the ... transit stop located in this center". Another example is the "Smart Growth" program promoted by the Environmental Protection Agency (EPA) to "Preserve open space, farmland, natural beauty, and critical environmental areas" (Keller & Burke, 2009).

15-Minute Cities

An even more recent reiteration of trying to entice people to live in the cities is the 15-Minute City. Joe Robison explained in his blog article, "One popular concept hailing from Paris is the 15-minute city. It's a city in which, wherever you live, everything you need is located within a 15-minute walk or bike ride away. While European in concept, many American cities such as Portland, Detroit, and Seattle are also looking for similar solutions. They endeavor to rebuild their cities into walkable, bikeable, and socially connected communities." (Robinson, 2023).

Urban Decline

With the history of people migrating from the country family farm into the cities, we have since seen a steady deterioration of those urban centers into slums of poverty and homelessness, and hotbeds of crime and insecurity for those living within these metropolises. We have also seen that there are mounting pressures for city-dwellers to pack closer and closer together with less need to travel or even own a car. Policy pressures are making it more difficult to find country property due to increased environmental regulations and large-scale farming operations.

The Peaceful Country Life

It is plain to see, that these once-inviting cities are increasingly evolving into hotbeds of crime and danger. The life we once envisioned in these beautiful cities is now cluttered with tent cities and seemingly endless graffiti. So, what is a person to do? Make plans to move out of the noise and din of the city into a peaceful life in the country!

References

Eighme, L. E. (1976). The Country Way. Southern Publishing.

Keeler, M., & Burke, B. (2009). Fundamentals of Integrated Design for Sustainable Building. US Green Building Council.

Robinson, J. (2023, August 15). Where are 15 Minute Cities Most Viable in the US? Movebuddha. Retrieved September 2, 2023, from https://www.movebuddha.com/blog/15-minute-cities/

Additional Video and Podcast Resources

Video Supplement to Chapter 1
www.preparingforthetimeoftrouble.com - Part 456
"Urban Dangers"

Chapter 2: The End of Life as We Know It

Most anyone can see that living in large cities is increasingly complex, fraught with dangers, littered with homeless tent city encampments and ever-present crime. Surprisingly, there have been forebodings and warnings in the past that many have not been aware of. The Bible, for instance, prophesies a time when it will be difficult to buy and sell. In the last book of the Bible, Revelation, John was given a vision portraying the future. "He was granted power to give breath to the image of the beast, that the image of the beast should both speak and cause as many as would not worship the image of the beast to be killed. He causes all, both small and great, rich and poor, free and slave, to receive a mark on their right hand or on their foreheads, and that no one may buy or sell except one who has the mark or the name of the beast, or the number of his name." Revelation 13:15-17 NKJV

The Future Foretold

This vision of the future was given to Jesus' disciple John, long after the crucifixion and transfiguration of Christ, when John was now an old man of about 90 years. He was imprisoned on a penal island and left to die. But Jesus came personally to him to provide him encouragement and a panoramic view of the distant future, including our present day. While this visit by Jesus to his longtime friend John was a happy reunion, the glimpse into the future included some ominous predictions of future troublous times.

The Magnificent Temple

Earlier in John's life, when he was a young man, he was with the other disciples and Jesus overlooking the magnificent Jewish temple in Jerusalem. This was the crown jewel, the pride of the people of Israel. Jesus shocked these disciples by stating that in a matter of three days, this grand temple would be destroyed with not one stone left upon another. In shocked amazement, John and his friends assumed that this was going to be the end of the world. "Then Jesus went out and departed from the temple, and His disciples came up to show Him the buildings of the temple. And Jesus said to them, 'Do you not see all these things? Assuredly, I say to you, not *one* stone shall be left here upon another, that shall not be thrown down.'" Matthew 24:1, 2 NKJV.

21

When Will These Things Be?

The disciples asked Jesus, "Tell us, when will these things be? And what will be the sign of Your coming, and of the end of the age?" Matthew 24:3 NKJV. You can see they thought that the destruction of the temple would be at Jesus's Second Coming and the end of the world as we know it. Jesus knew that the destruction of Jerusalem and the end of the world were two separate events thousands of years apart, but he predicted both events with one answer. In truth, the destruction of the temple and Jerusalem by the Romans happened 40 years later. Jesus's warning also foreshadowed the catastrophic events to happen at the end of our modern day, prior to His Second Coming.

The Time of Trouble

The tribulation or Time of Trouble would throw the world into unprecedented chaos and turmoil. Jesus had shared glimpses of this long before John's revelation. Over 500 years earlier, the prophet Daniel was likewise given a glimpse of the future, "And there shall be a Time of Trouble, such as never was since there was a nation, even to that time." Daniel 12:1 NKJV.

The Great Depression

As we have seen from the example of the Great Depression, those living in the cities endure much greater hardship during tough times than those in the country. John's vision even singled out cities as being in danger during the end-time Time of Trouble such as never was. "In the same hour there was a great earthquake, and a tenth of the city fell. In the earthquake seven thousand people were killed." Revelation 11:13. Later in the same vision, John was also shown that, "the cities of the nations fell." Revelation 16:19 NKJV.

Cities in Danger

So, it is evident from the Bible that cities are in danger in the final chapter of the history of this world. Some Bible commentators have expounded on the need to move out of the cities in preparation for avoiding some of these future troubles. In the book *Country Living*, author Ellen White drives the point home repeatedly. "Parents flock with their families to the cities, because they fancy it easier to obtain a livelihood there than in the country...Instead of the crowded city, seek some retired situation where your children will be, so far as possible, shielded from temptation, and there train and educate them for usefulness. The prophet Ezekiel thus enumerates the causes that led to Sodom's sin and destruction: 'Pride, fullness of bread, and abundance of idleness was in her and in her daughters; neither did she strengthen the hands of the poor and needy.' All who would escape the doom of Sodom, must shun the course that brought God's judgments upon that wicked city." (White, 1946).

The Time is Near

"The time is near when the large cities will be visited by the judgments of God... The ungodly cities of our world are to be swept away by the besom of destruction. In the calamities that are now befalling immense buildings and large portions of cities." (White, 1946).

Man Was Made to Live in the Country

God's original plan for mankind was for us to live in the country. The first home of Adam and Eve was in a garden...the Garden of Eden. It was not until Cain killed his brother Abel, that the concept of city dwelling was born. "And Cain knew his wife, and she conceived and bore Enoch. And he built a city, and called the name of the city after the name of his son—Enoch." Genesis 4:17 NKJV.

The First City

That first city of Enoch was the forerunner to future cities, including the famed city of Babylon. That city was built in rebellion to God following the worldwide flood. Genesis 11:3, 4. The Tower of Babel was erected to provide a way of escape from the fear of another worldwide flood. This was despite God promising not to do that again, symbolized by the rainbow as a reminder. History is fraught with stories of large cities and their evil and crime, including Sodom and Gomorrah. While God did not bring on the world a global flood, He did give warnings against the evils of large cities.

Fire from Heaven

Sodom and Gomorrah were destroyed by fire from heaven. "Then the LORD rained brimstone and fire on Sodom and Gomorrah, from the LORD out of the heavens." Genesis 19:24 NKJV. It does seem possible that God's forbearance with the evil cities in our day could end again in being destroyed by earthquakes or fireballs from the heavens, as has been visualized. One does not need to just depend on the predictions of future destruction of the cities to have reason to consider a move to the country.

Strategic Relocation Book Cover image used with permission from Joel Skousen

Joel Skousen, in his book *Strategic Relocation: North American Guide to Safe Places*, analyzes various regions globally, but especially in North America. He identifies areas that are in danger such as large cities and even some places in the wide open, such as parts of Montana and North Dakota due to the proliferation of nuclear silos. Here is what he has to say about the dangers of big cities, "As we have repeatedly warned, we see inherent dangers in all large population centers and recommend people move away from these areas if at all possible." (Skousen, 2013).

Nuclear Targets Map image used with permission from Joel Skousen

Most anyone can see that living in the large cities is increasingly complex, fraught with dangers including natural disasters, plus littered with homeless tent city encampments and ever-present crime. So, when is a good time to leave the cities and move into the quietness and solitude of country living? The sooner the better!

References

The New King James Version, 2020, Revelation 13:15-17.

The New King James Version, 2020, Matthew 24:1-3.

The New King James Version, 2020, Daniel 12:1.

The New King James Version, 2020, Revelation 16:19.

White, E. G. (1946). *Country Living* (p. 5). Review and Herald Publishing Association.

White, E. G. (1946). *Country Living* (p. 7). Review and Herald Publishing Association.

The New King James Version, 2020, Genesis 4:17.

The New King James Version, 2020, Genesis 11:3, 4.

The New King James Version, 2020, Genesis 19:24.

Skousen, J. M. (2013). *Strategic Relocation: North American Guide to Safe Places,* (3rd ed., p. 118). Printing Resource

Additional Video and Podcast Resources

Video Supplement to Chapter 2
www.preparingforthetimeoftrouble.com- Part 457
"The End of Life as We Know It"

Chapter 3: When to Leave the Cities

As discussed in the previous chapter, Joel Skousen, in his book *Strategic Relation: North American Guide to Safe Places*, admonishes, "As we have repeatedly warned, we see inherent dangers in all large population centers and recommend people move away from these areas if at all possible." (Skousen, 2013). The motivators for those yearning to leave the cities and move into the country can include a variety of negative factors in the cities, but it was not until the COVID-19 pandemic that this migration was seen to escalate. As noted in a National Public Radio analysis of the trend, they stated, "When the pandemic was in full force, one of the big news storylines was that families were fleeing cities for the countryside or the suburbs." (Wamsley, 2023).

Couple Moving image used by permission from Economic Innovation Group

Outmigration from the Cities

An article published by the U.S. Census on March 30, 2023, documented the movement of families from the cities to the suburbs and countryside during the COVID-19 pandemic. "The COVID-19 pandemic changed the U.S. population in many ways, including births, deaths, and international migration. One of its more intriguing impacts was on domestic migration patterns.

Migration Trends

Some longstanding trends accelerated, such as outmigration from large urban areas in the Northeast, while other trends reversed, resulting in some small rural counties gaining rather than losing population." (Rogers, 2023). In an article on the Economic Innovation Group's website entitled *Young Families Have Not Returned to Large Cities Post-Pandemic*, Connor O'Brien states, "The exodus of young families from the country's major urban areas continued into 2022, even as the economy began to normalize." (O'Brien, 2023).

The Move to Idaho

One such rural area that saw a massive influx of people moving into the country was the state of Idaho. This domestic migration was not only seen among young, working families who now could work remotely, but also older people who could afford to pay cash for their home in Idaho. Many times, a motivating factor was the increasing liberal changes in governmental policies and limitations of its citizens. One such factor had to do with the resistance by some to taking the COVID-19 vaccine. In some liberal states, public employees such as medical personnel, state workers, teachers, and police officers were mandated to take the jab or lose their jobs. Many chose to relocate to areas such as Idaho which not only did not have such requirements but often did not even require masks, while most of the world did.

Supply and Demand

There have been many personal testimonies of long-time residents of Idaho who began to be priced out being able to continue to live where their families had for generations. With many average people working at minimum wages, they found themselves not earning enough to live in their beloved state of Idaho. This was the result of the mass migrations of affluent people from other states such as California moving into the area. Supply and demand escalated the housing prices. If these locals did not cash in and move away, they would find themselves with higher property taxes due to increased assessed values.

Family Leaving City image used by permission from Economic Innovation Group

Reverse Migration

Time will tell how many of these families who rushed to move to the wilderness of Idaho, will choose to stay permanently. Some will have come from warmer climates, and with buying on a sunny summer day in Idaho, did not realize how harsh and long-lasting the winters can be. No doubt, many will become disillusioned and move back in regret. Others, who were able to work remotely during the pandemic, may find themselves being forced to relocate to report physically to their place of employment. It will be interesting to see how the ebb and flow of Idaho migration ends up in the long run.

Struggling Financially

One factor that became evident was that those who had been wishing to move out of the city into the countryside of Idaho found it increasingly a struggle financially due to the skyrocketing prices of homes and land because of the rush of supply and demand during the pandemic. The takeaway seems to be that a person should plan carefully when and how to move into the country, to avoid poor choices in a rush to judgment. Careful planning and appropriate decisions about how and when to move into the country can increase the chances of that move being a benefit for the short and long term.

Reasons to Leave the Cities

The author of the book *Country Living* gave many reasons to leave the cities and move to the country. These included allowing children to run free of danger and negative distractions as well as the health and well-being of people of any age. "If in the providence of God, we can secure places away from the cities, the Lord would have us do this. There are troublous times before us." (White, 1946).

Cultivation on Country Property

Further detail is given such as, "The time has come, when, as God opens the way, families should move out of the cities. The children should be taken into the country. The parents should get as suitable a place as their means will allow. Though the dwelling may be small, yet there should be land in connection with it, that may be cultivated." (White, 1946).

Mark of the Beast

An even more compelling reason to move out of the cities into the country is that the Bible predicts a time in the future when those who do not accept the mark of the beast will be prevented from buying or selling. In the last book of the Bible, Revelation, John was given a vision portraying the future. "He was granted power to give breath to the image of the beast, that the image of the beast should both speak and cause as many as would not worship the image of the beast to be killed. He causes all, both small and great, rich and poor, free and slave, to receive a mark on their right hand or on their foreheads, and that no one may buy or sell except one who has the mark or the name of the beast, or the number of his name." Revelation 13:15-17 NKJV

No Buy, No Sell

The question is, if a person could not buy or sell, how much harder would it be living in the congestion of the cities, as compared to living in the country? The book *Country Living* once again provides a motivation to move into the county, "Again and again the Lord has instructed that our people are to take their families away from the cities, into the country, where they can raise their own provisions; for in the future the problem of buying and selling will be a very serious one. We should now begin to heed the instruction given us over and over again." (White, 1946).

EMP Threats

Beside the overall well-being of one's family and planning to be self-sustaining during hard times, there looms another threat. The threat of an EMP or Electromagnetic Pulse. This is a high-altitude detonation of a nuclear bomb, potentially taking down the grid and wiping out most electronic devices. Any serious entity wishing to do harm to the USA could likely do a first strike using an EMP. Even North Korea has publicly threatened to do this to the USA. While there will be an in-depth look at the topic of EMPs later in this book, the point being made here is that while an EMP would affect everyone, the crippling effects would be exponentially more serious for those not living a self-sustaining lifestyle in the country. In 2012, there was a hearing before Congress regarding the threat and impact of an EMP on the homeland. They reported to Congress that, "The immediate and eventual impact, directly and indirectly, on the human population, especially in major cities, *is unthinkable*." (Lungren, 2012). You can see from the point of view of this commission on Homeland Security, the crippling impacts of an EMP and the grid going down would likely be much more difficult for those living in the cities.

Laying Plans to be Self-Sufficient

We may not know in advance when we could encounter the crippling effects of an EMP. It would behoove us to lay plans to be more self-sufficient and independent of services we currently have at our fingertips. There may be a time when we will be unable to access and spend our financial resources. Moving into a country setting could provide us with the ability to grow our own food. These types of preparations could be favorable and possibly have life-saving benefits when times get tough.

References

Wamsley, L. (2023, July 9). *Young families continued to leave cities last year – but at a slower pace*. NPR. https://www.npr.org/2023/07/09/1186483034/family-exodus-cities-census-data

Rogers, L. (2023, March 30). *Domestic outmigration from some urban counties slowed, smaller gains in rural counties*. Census.gov. https://www.census.gov/library/stories/2023/03/domestic-migration-trends-shifted.html

O'Brien, C. (2023, June 29). *Young families have not returned to large cities post-pandemic*. Economic Innovation Group. https://eig.org/2023-family-exodus/

White, E. G. (1946). *Country Living* (p. 20). Review and Herald Publishing Association.

White, E. G. (1946). *Country Living* (p. 24). Review and Herald Publishing Association.

White, E. G. (1946). *Country Living* (p. 9). Review and Herald Publishing Association.

Lungren, D. E. (2012, September 12). *EMP Threat: Examining the Consequences*. The EMP threat: Examining the consequences. https://www.govinfo.gov/content/pkg/CHRG-112hhrg80856/html/CHRG-112hhrg80856.htm

Additional Video and Podcast Resources

Video Supplement to Chapter 3
www.preparingforthetimeoftrouble.com - Part 458
"When to Leave the Cities"

Chapter 4: What if You Can't Buy or Sell?

We likely have all heard of China's Social Credit System. This involves the use of half a billion surveillance cameras to monitor the Chinese population. With the use of facial recognition capabilities, the system has the potential to categorize individuals into social groups based on that person's activities. Amanda Lee wrote an article for the South China Morning Post. She explained, "Total surveillance has only been possible in the last ten years as algorithms have become more sophisticated at sifting large data files. Of the world's 1 billion surveillance cameras in use, *half* are in China. Almost all these cameras are equipped with facial recognition software so that identity can be matched to an image on any camera at any time." (Lee, 2020).

Chinese Social Credit System image used with permission from Simon Black, www.sovereignman.com

Population Profiling

A Mind Matters article by Heather Zeiger explained, "The Chinese government's eventual goal is a centralized comprehensive profile on every person in China that can be accessed by any government official at any time. These profiles are built from three interconnected sources: data retrieved from surveillance cameras equipped with facial recognition technology, hidden smartphone trackers, and biometric information collected from every citizen, regardless of criminal record." (Zeiger, 2022)

Authoritarian Rule

The New York Times did an intensive investigation into video surveillance in China. An article highlighting the main takeaways stated that "The Chinese government's goal is clear: designing a system to maximize what the state can find out about a person's identity, activities and social connections, which could ultimately help the government maintain its authoritarian rule." (Qian, 2022).

Phone-Tracking

The article went on to claim "Phone-tracking devices are now everywhere. The police are creating some of the largest DNA databases in the world. And the authorities are building upon facial recognition technology to collect voice prints from the general public." (Qian, 2022). This kind of activity in a totalitarian country on the other side of the world might seem to have no effect on those of us who live in the USA. Things have changed since the attack on 911. The subsequent development of the Homeland Security Council in the month following 911 was done by an executive order of George W. Bush.

Collecting Personal Data

Many believe that Homeland Security is responsible for gathering unprecedented quantities of personal data of all US citizens. This government entitlement opens the door to the possibility of collecting cellphone conversations, locations of and emergency alerts to all mobile devices, as well as gathering email and text information.

Travel Control

More and more we are seeing traffic cameras reading vehicle license plates. True, many times these keep track of toll road charges and catching speeding drivers. Is it possible that this technology could eventually be used to control where you might travel? One might wonder what the real purpose is for those black digital signs above many highways in America. True, they are used for emergency traffic information and amber alerts, but might it be possible that these programmable signs could eventually be used for controlling travel during times of martial law?

Restrictive America

We can see how advances in technology have enhanced our lives with smartphones, global positioning system (GPS), entry door cameras as well as smart TVs and appliances. But is all this technology paving the way for a more restrictive America? If the Bible's prediction of a time to come when some will not be allowed to buy or sell, could these technologies be poised to enable these restrictions?

Problem of Buying and Selling

As stated previously, the book *Country Living* provides a motivation to move into the country, "Again and again the

Lord has instructed that our people are to take their families away from the cities, into the country, where they can raise their own provisions; for in the future, the problem of buying and selling will be a very serious one. We should now begin to heed the instruction given us over and over again." (White, 1946). Back when this statement was made, there were fewer modern conveniences and technological advances. While living in the country back then, life would have been simpler and growing food was the primary concern.

Supply-Chain Problems

But now, let's think about what the impact would be on our modern lifestyles if we could not buy or sell. It is understood that if the conveniences we are used to were no longer at our disposal, terrible things would happen in short order. Thinking about our food, what if the trucks could not get fuel due to the power grid being down? The grocery store shelves would be bare in a matter of a few days, if not sooner. Just think about the rush for products such as disinfectant wipes and toilet paper at Costco during the pandemic. One time, my wife went to her favorite grocery store early in the day and found the produce aisles empty. Upon inquiring of the produce manager why the shelves were bare, she was told that the truck had not made deliveries yet that day. Being as our family had just been discussing the implications of a grid-down scenario, this was a wake-up call for us. All it took was one day for the shelves of produce to empty out! What would the impact be of long-term shortages?

EMP Impacts

What if all outside services came to a sudden halt due to an EMP taking out the grid? No fuel. No food. Municipal water supplies would eventually drain to empty. Sewage systems would back up. Hospitals could not provide most services. Nights would be totally dark with no lights. It would not take any time at all until there would be widespread looting and violence in the streets. Once again, those in the cities would be most vulnerable and helpless.

Self-Reflecting

So, let's do some self-reflection. If you could not buy or sell, or if all outside services were no longer available due to an EMP attack, what areas of your life would be in crisis? The seemingly insignificant experience, years ago, of seeing empty produce shelves motivated our family do this self-reflection. We then came to the realization that *everything* we needed daily required pulling out the wallet. This was a real turning point for our family, and we began making plans to attempt to "Get out of Dodge" and move toward a more sustainable country lifestyle. It seems like it would be a smart move for each person to begin to work towards a life with backup plans for independence and sustainability, rather than procrastinate only to find oneself caught unprepared and vulnerable. Now is the time to make those life choices and start the journey toward a sustainable country life.

References

Lee, A. (2020, December 15). *What is China's Social Credit System and why is it controversial?* South China Morning Post. https://www.scmp.com/economy/china-economy/article/3096090/what-chinas-social-credit-system-and-why-it-controversial

Zeiger, H. (2022, July 1). *China is quite serious about total surveillance of every citizen*. Mind Matters. https://mindmatters.ai/2022/07/china-is-quite-serious-about-total-surveillance-of-every-citizen/

Qian, I., Xiao, M., Mozur, P., & Cardia, A. (2022, June 21). *Four takeaways from a Times investigation into China's expanding Surveillance State*. The New York Times. https://www.nytimes.com/2022/06/21/world/asia/china-surveillance-investigation.html

White, E. G. (1946). *Country Living* (p. 9). Review and Herald Publishing Association.

Additional Video and Podcast Resources

Video Supplement to Chapter 4
www.preparingforthetimeoftrouble.com - Part 459
"What If You Can't Buy or Sell"

www.preparingforthetimeoftrouble.com - Part 60
"EMP Dangers and Prevention"

Chapter 5: Planning for Being Sustainably Independent

Setting the Stage

Assuming by now you are convinced to move out of the city, we will quickly consider how country living will be different than urban life. One might like to think that living in the country is sitting on a porch all day, looking at the beautiful scenery. While the scenery will be beautiful, it is not a life of leisure. Country living requires additional responsibilities that a city dweller is not needing to be concerned about such as gardening, storing up firewood, as well as developing and maintaining the property, just to name a few of the obvious ones. Once a person gets into the rhythm of daily chores, the tendency for some is to try to do it all! Like Lloyd Eighme so aptly stated in his book *The Country Way,* don't try to complete in a short period of time what it took your grandparents a lifetime to accomplish. (Eighme, 1976). Take time to enjoy the journey. That chair with a view is on that porch for a reason.

The Foundation

Whether you are going to move or have already moved into the country, the rest of this book will be a great resource about each of the various aspects that are involved in country living which are different from city dwelling.

Being Self-Sustaining

With the likely future interruption to our way of living, we would all do well to review what various aspects we need in our daily lives. Which of these require us to pull our wallet out? What backup plans might we put into place to be proactive in anticipation of any unforeseen interruption to normal living?

Being Off-Grid

One way to look at this is to consider what is meant by "being off-grid". For most, being off-grid means not using the power grid. For others, being off the grid means hiding from society and government overreach. But yet another way to think of things is being disconnected from any of those outside services we pay for and depend on.

Escaping Traditional Monetary System

An organization named "Woodpackers" suggests some ways to live off the grid without money, by explaining that, "by engaging in work exchanges, joining eco-villages or building your own sustainable life from scratch, it's possible to escape traditional monetary systems while fostering personal growth and environmental conservation." (Woodpackers, 2023). They identify some key ways to embark on a self-sufficient life: "find low-cost or free land; grow your own food; fish responsibly; forage for edible plants; collect and filter water; generate energy through renewable means; swap goods and services; and find alternative income means." (Woodpackers, 2023).

Uncle Sam Encourages Gardening circa 1917 image source: Library of Congress

Three Life Support Requirements

Another way to look at this is to do some self-reflection to identify what specific items you purchase. There are three main things we need just to be alive: air, water, and food. It is generally believed that a person can live 3 weeks without food, 3 days without water, and 3 minutes without breathing. In an overall sense, the air we breathe is free for the taking, so we will not be concerned about that one. But all of the rest of our needs are not free.

Water Grid – Safe Water Sources

During my youth, I believed that water was free. When the bottled water craze started, I could not understand why anyone would pay for water. Now we carry Costco bottled water in each of our vehicles. Whether your domestic water source is municipal water in the city or from a well in the country, it is not completely free – there will be a bill to pay for the city water or electricity to operate the well pump. Even rainwater catchment would require filtering to safely drink the water. In a strict off-grid analysis of water, one would benefit from purchasing ahead of time some water filters to at least allow them to retrieve drinking water from a creek or lake.

Food Grid – Year-Round Food Sources

We all buy food. In an analysis of how we could position ourselves to not have to purchase food, there are a variety of preplanning efforts that would need to be considered. The various aspects of this important need will be discussed at length later in this book. But for now, let's look at the topic from a hands-off vantage point. What planning you would need to do to have your food needs met year-round would depend on what you eat. If you are a plant-based vegan vegetarian, then the garden would be your main source of food. For those that are lacto ovo vegetarians, being as they additionally eat eggs and dairy products, there would be a need for chickens and a cow or goat to milk. Besides raising chickens for harvesting eggs daily, there might be the need to have a rooster in order to have some eggs hatch with chicks to expand the flock. If you are a carnivore, you will need a source of meat. This could be from raising birds and animals as well as fishing and hunting game. Your type of diet you have will indicate what sources of food you would need. None of these food products will last indefinitely without some form of preservation. These methods could include water-bath canning, drying, freeze drying, smoking, pickling, and freezing, to name a few. Each of these will be discussed in more detail later in another chapter.

Power Grid - Alternative Power Generation

Besides these three life-support requirements, there are many things we purchase that would not be available in a grid-down or no buy/no sell scenario. Most people think of alternative power generation when they hear the term "off-grid". If a person chooses to not connect to the power grid or if it is impractical or impossible, then there are some other ways one can generate power.

An article by Daniel Hosfeld, titled "Off Grid Electricity: What You Need to Know", identifies some examples of ways to generate electricity off-grid. Some examples of ways to generate electric energy off the grid: "Solar (such as photovoltaics) generally using solar panels. Wind using a wind turbine (windmill) to turn a generator for your power. Geothermal which is basically heat extraction from the earth. Micro-hydro using the natural flow of water." (Hosfeld, 2022). CNET contributor, Michelle Starr, even suggests the option of using your muscles riding a bike to power small electrical devices such as a laptop. (Starr, 2013). We will explore each of these in more detail later in the book.

But beyond the most common definition of alternative energy having to do with generating electricity, there are many other types of "grids" on which we depend. If we are going to really be off-grid we need to consider these other areas on which we depend.

Heat Grid – Burning Firewood

It sure is nice to simply set the thermostat to the desired temperature, and forget about it, right? Whether your heat is provided by the use of electricity, propane, or natural gas, it all takes paying a bill. Of course, that is also the case for air conditioning. So, what alternative method of heating is there that requires very little or no money? Trees of course! If you live on property that has trees, some of them can be harvested each year to provide firewood to burn in a wood stove in the house. There is nothing like the radiant heat provided by a crackling fire in a stove! Gathering firewood is very labor-intensive and generally requires the use of a chainsaw, fuel, and oil. What if you could not buy fuel and oil? Then the alternative would be to do it all manually with an axe, handsaws, splitting maul, and hatchet. Do you have any of these tools and do you know how to use them? Might it be a good time to learn?

Information Grid – Old School Face-to-face Communication

So much of our activities, transactions, and personal interactions are based on technology. We share and retrieve information by talking on our phones, texting, faxing documents, or transferring videos or large files via drop boxes. We participate in remote meetings using Skype or Zoom. Gone are the days of three TV networks. Now we often don't even subscribe to a TV cable service, rather watching news, TV shows, and movies are by means of streaming media services such as Netflix or a growing number of other such providers. We access the Internet through ISPs via cable, DSL, fiber optics, or satellite dish systems. Some cell service providers offer unlimited data plans for smartphones, allowing access to the Internet or online streaming services with complete mobility anywhere, any time. What would be a backup plan for a possible time when there would be no information grid? Maybe ham radios or even communicating with others face-to-face?

Financial Grid – Cashless Society

Most of us use the current banking system in a variety of ways. We not only deposit and spend cash, use debit, and credit cards, access ATM machines, plus we usually have some form of savings or investments. All these transactions require interfacing with financial institutions. If you no longer had access to these monetary establishments, how would you exchange money? Of course, there is that proverbial scenario of hiding money under your mattress, which would preferably be done by using a safe in a secured location. Another avenue worth considering in preparation for hard times is purchasing some gold or silver coins. It is assumed that during a time when you can't use money, you could trade with precious metals. The problem I see is how do you have a silver coin in the right monetary value to exchange for a small item such as a loaf of bread. During the Great Depression, often times those without money used some form of bartering. "Can I trade this for that?"

Medical Grid – Homestead Remedies and Medicinal Plants

Today we depend on the medical system for help in emergencies or for general health and wellness maintenance. What would you do if you did not have access to any medical services or medications? That would be a good time to have learned ahead of time about herbal remedies. In the pioneering days of America, there were rarely any medical services, especially if a person lived remotely. Unlike in the past, the doctors of today do not make house calls. It seems important now to learn about herbal medicinal plants and natural remedies.

Self-Reflection

It seems obvious that the most significant takeaway is that we pay for almost everything we do in our technologically advanced modern lifestyle. If our ability to purchase these services vanished overnight, how prepared would you be? No doubt most of us would do well to start doing some self-reflection and lay plans to create backup options for each of these things we depend on so much in our daily lives.

References

Eighme, L. E. (1976). The Country Way. Southern Publishing.

Worldpackers. (2023, September 1). *How to live off the grid with no money: A practical guide*. How to Live Off the Grid with No Money: A Practical Guide. https://www.worldpackers.com/articles/how-to-live-off-the-grid-with-no-money

Hosfeld, D. (2022, June 25). *Off grid electricity: What you need to know*. An Off Grid Life. https://www.anoffgridlife.com/off-grid-electricity-what-you-need-to-know/

Starr, M. (2013, November 19). *Pedal power: Pedal your desk to power your laptop*. Pedal Power: pedal your desk to power your laptop. https://www.cnet.com/home/kitchen-and-household/pedal-power-pedal-your-desk-to-power-your-laptop/

Additional Video and Podcast Resources

Video Supplement to Chapter 5
www.preparingforthetimeoftrouble.com - Part 461
"Planning for Being Sustainably Independent"

www.preparingforthetimeoftrouble.com - Part 178
"What Does It Mean to be Off Grid?"

Chapter 6: Power Grid - Alternative Energy: The Basics

Most of the time, alternative power energy systems make power by using renewable sources, such as the sun, wind, and water. National Grid Group is a large corporation that has power production facilities in the United States and the United Kingdom. They explain it this way, "Renewable energy is energy that comes from a source that won't run out. They are natural and self-replenishing, and usually have a low- or zero-carbon footprint. Examples of renewable energy sources include wind power, solar power, bioenergy (organic matter burned as a fuel) and hydroelectric, including tidal energy." (National Grid, 2023).

Solar Panel image source: Pixabay

While there are several options for alternative energy power generation methods, for the most part, they all utilize some common components. We will address each of these important areas in an attempt to explain the basics in simple terms to make it easy to understand.

AC and DC Electricity

There are two kinds of electricity in any alternative energy system: alternating current (AC), or direct current (DC). Alternating current is the kind of power you have in your house. A toaster, for instance, runs on AC power. Things that run on batteries, such as flashlights and cell phones, use DC power. Most of the alternative energy methods will start by making DC power. That is the case for solar, wind, hydro, and pedal power.

Direct Current

Simply put, direct current electricity flows in one direction constantly. This is done with a power wire and a ground wire. The electricity flows from the plus side (the power wire) to the negative side (the ground wire).

Alternating Current

By comparison, alternating current has a plus side and a neutral side, but the power jumps up and down much like an ocean wave. When a wave comes toward shore, it is followed by no wave, which could be thought of as a negative wave. That up-and-down action is called a cycle. The number of cycles for an ocean wave might be one or two per minute. But in alternating current electricity, it is 60 cycles per second. DC power can be stored in batteries, while AC cannot be stored for later use.

Wind Power image used with permission from Backwoods Solar

Wind and Hydroelectric Power

Wind power turbines and hydroelectric dams work similarly, in that they produce alternating current. Because alternating current cannot be stored for later use, the water flowing through the hydroelectric dam adjusts based on the need for power. In a similar manner, a commercial wind power generator will speed up or slow down based on the power grid's demand at that moment. This is why if you have seen a wind farm in action, such as in Palm Springs, California, some wind generators will be turning, and others may be stopped. When I first saw this phenomenon, I thought it was because some of the wind generators were not working and needed to be repaired. But the reason was that the wind farm made adjustments based on the grid's power demands at that moment. For instance, if everyone in Los Angeles turned on their air conditioners at the same time, the wind turbines would speed up to match the need at that moment.

Lack of Power Storage

There is one serious problem with wind generators and hydroelectric dams – the lack of being able to store power. If the wind stops in the nighttime, and Los Angeles power demand increases at night due to lighting, then the wind generators cannot keep up. This is why they have more wind generators than are needed. It sure would be great if there was a way to store up that power for those non-windy days!

Batteries

Batteries store direct current electricity. Solar panels produce DC power. Other forms of off-grid, alternative power generation methods, such as small wind turbines, and micro-hydro systems, plus even pedal power, all make direct current electricity. Therefore, any of those approaches to making electricity can store that power in batteries. While large-scale power generating methods such as hydroelectric dams and wind farms, cannot store power for later use.

Power Storage Capacity

When considering off-grid power generating options, batteries are helpful because off-grid systems are DC. To maintain the charge on the batteries to an appropriate level, there is a need for a device to control the power to the batteries. The problem might be that one of these power-generating devices might make too much electricity for the battery to be able to store. Batteries have a limit on their storage capacity. To store more power, you need either larger batteries or battery bank.

Charge Controllers

A "charge controller" is designed to adjust the flow of electricity going to the battery and to stop sending power when the battery is full. When the battery gets low, the charge controller allows more electricity to be sent into the battery. One big benefit of a charge controller is that it protects the battery from being damaged by over-charging. Backwoods Solar is a major supplier of off-grid power-generating components. They explain it this way, "A charge controller regulates the power from solar, wind, or hydro which goes to the battery. To prevent battery damage from overcharging, the charge controller automatically cuts back, stops, or diverts the charge when batteries become full." (Backwoods, 2023).

Power Inverter

Now you can generate electricity on a sunny day and store that power in the battery so you can have some lights day or night. The problem is that the toaster does not run on DC power. It needs AC power. For that matter, the lights in your house are also AC. So, somehow, we need to convert that DC power to AC, since everything in your house runs on AC power. This brings us to the other important device in an alternative energy system – the "Power Inverter".

Useful Household Power

A power inverter changes DC power to AC power and does it in such a way that your household items can be at the correct voltage. That toaster is 110 volts. Typical power inverters will also output 220 volts for larger household items such as an oven or clothes dryer. Backwoods Solar defines it this way, "The inverter is the major electronic component of a power system. It converts DC power stored in batteries to 120-volt AC, standard household power." Backwoods, 2023).

Basic Components

We now have a way to make power (solar panel), batteries to store that power for later use, a charge controller to keep those batteries safe, and an inverter to convert that power into power that can be used in your house. No matter how large or small an off-grid power-generating system is, it likely has those basic components. The same would be true if the power was generated from wind using a wind turbine or making electricity from flowing water by way of a micro-hydro generator. Each of these methods will utilize these basic components.

References

National Grid. (2023). *What are the different types of renewable energy?*. National Grid Group. https://www.nationalgrid.com/stories/energy-explained/what-are-different-types-renewable-energy

Backwoods, *A simple explanation*. Backwoods Solar. (2023, May 19). https://backwoodssolar.com/learning-center/learning-center-a-simplified-explanation/

Backwoods, *A simple explanation*. Backwoods Solar. (2023, May 19). https://backwoodssolar.com/learning-center/learning-center-a-simplified-explanation/

Additional Video and Podcast Resources

www.preparingforthetimeoftrouble.com - Part 28 "Alternative Energy: Understanding Solar Power Systems"

Chapter 7: Power Grid - Alternative Energy: Solar

The most popular form of alternative energy is solar due to several factors. For one, there are no moving parts to maintain, as compared to wind or micro hydro systems. Another difference between solar and other forms of alternative energy is that solar does not use a generator. An important benefit of solar is cost. Solar panel prices have dropped and become more efficient over the years. A disadvantage of solar is it only generates power during daylight hours.

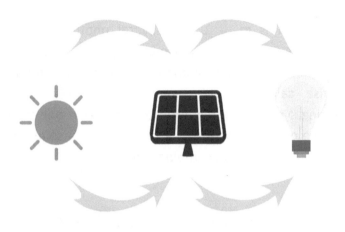

Solar Power image source: Pixabay

How it Works

The process of capturing electrical energy from the sun is unique to solar alone. How does a solar panel generate electricity from the sun? The U.S. Energy Information Administration explains it this way, "A photovoltaic (PV) cell, commonly called a solar cell, is a nonmechanical device that converts sunlight directly into electricity. Some PV cells can convert artificial light into electricity...Sunlight is composed of photons, or particles of solar energy...When photons strike a PV cell...the absorbed photons provide energy to generate electricity... Electrical conductors on the cell absorb the electrons. When the conductors are connected in an electrical circuit to an external load, such as a battery, electricity flows through the circuit." (EIA, 2023).

A solar panel is made up of several photovoltaic cells arranged in a pattern. The image below shows a single cell on the left, then cells combine into a solar module otherwise called a solar panel. Usually, solar power generating systems are made up of more than one panel. The image on the right shows an example of a solar array with nine solar panels in combination.

Alternative Energy image source: Pixabay

Backwoods Solar, a major distributor of off-grid power components explains, "The amount of power a solar array produces depends on the number of modules you use and the number of daily sunshine hours in your climate. Overcast days with only half normal brightness give half of normal power. Some climates allow much more power in summer than in winter. Solar modules for off-grid solar systems can easily be added to your array to increase power as your needs grow. Solar panels are rated by watts, volts, and amps. The watt rating is the best indicator of the charging you get and is what you will see on your meter during ideal sun conditions." (Backwoods, 2023).

A solar array, made up of a grouping of solar panels, is mounted on the roof of a building or mounted on a rack on the ground. Either method would be oriented to take advantage of the largest amount of sun exposure throughout the day. This means the panels would be pointed in the right direction east to west, with the panels angled to match the sun's location compared to the horizon. It is also important to locate the solar array to avoid shadows from trees or buildings.

Solar Panels image used by permission from Backwoods Solar

Solar Effectiveness

Solar panels come in different sizes and power capacities. According to solar.com, "Today, the most common power rating is 400 Watts as it provides a good balance of efficiency and affordability. A 400-Watt panel with 4.5 direct sun hours a day can be expected to produce 1,800 Watt-hours of DC electricity per day — or roughly 1,750 Watt-hours once it's converted to AC electricity — which is more than enough to power a refrigerator and lighting needs for the average US household." (Ost, 2023).

When deciding if installing a solar power system is going to work, some might say that your area of the country won't work because of having too many overcast days. Or they might claim that solar doesn't work in the rain. Neither is correct, although it is a fact that while direct sunlight can provide full power generating potential, the less sunny times will generate less power compared to full sun, but usually produce some electricity. Consequently, when deciding on how large a solar system you might need, one should factor for those overcast days, by compensating with additional panels. That way the system will be designed for most weather situations.

Peak Sun Hours

Peak sun hours are the times of day when the full, direct sun is available on the panels. Chi Odogwu, in a CNET article, offers this helpful information, "There are several online tools available that can help you calculate the peak sun hours at your home, including the National Renewable Energy Laboratory's PVWatts Calculator and the European Commission's Photovoltaic Geographical Information System (PVGIS)." (Odogwu, 2023).

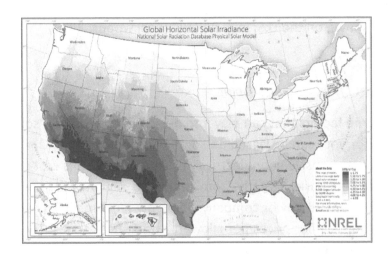

Solar Irradiance Map image source: National Renewable
Energy Laboratory

Calculating the Size of System Needed

Backwoods Solar (www.backwoodsolar.com) offers a free
catalog either in print or in PDF format for download. This is
not only a catalog but a great book explaining almost
everything you need to know to design your system,
including charts and forms to help you document your
power needs in your house and calculate the subsequent
size of a solar power system. Backwoods will also design
your system based on the information from those forms as
a free service. And if you decide to purchase the
components from them, they will provide free phone
support before, during, and long after the installation.
"Since all locations have different amounts of sunny days,

we must add a percentage to make up for cloudy, short winter days. The percentage to add for areas in the 48 states is shown on the U.S. map below." (Backwoods, 2023).

Cost Effectiveness of Solar

Some factors that can play into deciding if investing is solar is for you, can be based on some additional factors. One is how expensive your electricity is in your area. This cost per kilowatt varies greatly from region to region and power company to power company. Some power companies even charge higher prices per kilowatt during peak times. There was a region in the U.S., that as a result of efforts for that state to invest in fighting climate change and moving toward more renewable energy, that the prices of electricity in that area doubled in a very short period of time.

Conclusion

Check the details carefully when deciding what solar power system to install.

References

EIA. (2023, May 26). *U.S. Energy Information Administration - EIA - independent statistics and analysis*. Photovoltaics and electricity - U.S. Energy Information Administration (EIA). https://www.eia.gov/energyexplained/solar/photovoltaics-and-electricity.php

Backwoods. (2023). *Backwoods Solar*. https://backwoodssolar.com/product-category/default-category/products/solar-panels-1/

Ost, I. (2023, August 17). *How much energy does a solar panel produce?*. Solar.com. https://www.solar.com/learn/how-much-energy-does-a-solar-panel-produce/

Odogwu, C. (2023, August 18). *This is how much sunlight your solar panel system needs*. CNET. https://www.cnet.com/home/energy-and-utilities/peak-sun-hours/

Backwoods. (2022). *Backwoods Solar Catalog and Planning Guise, page 9*. Backwoods Solar.

Additional Video and Podcast Resources

www.preparingforthetimeoftrouble.com - Part 28
"Alternative Energy: Understanding Solar Power Systems"

www.preparingforthetimeoftrouble.com - Part 36
"Alternative Energy: Solar Power Systems Tour"

Chapter 8: Power Grid - Alternative Energy: Wind

There are times when wind power generation is worth considering. Many times, people install a wind turbine without adequate research and are very disappointed with the results. It is recommended to start with solar power and record the wind speed carefully throughout the whole year. This data will help you establish if it is justified to invest in and depend on wind power generation.

Wind Speed Requirements

While a minimum of 8 miles per hour is required to even begin to make power using wind, it is recommended that your location would yield an *average* of 12-15 miles per hour year-round in order to warrant using wind. (Backwoods, 2022). The reality is that there are very few locations where that kind of consistent wind is available. If it is, it may not be a very enjoyable place to live.

Wind Alternative Energy image source: Pixabay

Large commercial wind turbines have basically the same components as residential-size systems. This illustration below shows that there are blades that turn and power the generator. Pretty simple in concept but can be complicated.

Weakness of Mechanical Components

Unlike solar power, wind power uses mechanical, moving parts. Therefore, they can break and require ongoing maintenance. This is complicated by the fact that in order for the turbine to work properly, it most often is mounted high on a pole or tower. This is difficult because maintenance or repair of the turbine requires accessing the equipment at the top of the tower. This is not only scary but dangerous.

Wind Generator image source: Pixabay

Marine Wind Turbines

One place where a wind turbine is often used successfully, is on a boat. There are two reasons why this might be a good option on a sailboat or yacht. The first is that the open water lends itself to having wind. The second reason is that a boat needs very little electrical power generated. These marine wind turbines are usually affordable and easy to mount on the boat.

Marine Wind Power System image used with permission from Backwoods Solar

Residential Wind Power Systems

For those wishing to include a residential wind power system, the turbine needs to be at least 30 feet above any trees or buildings in the vicinity. It is also recommended that the wind turbine be at least 300 feet away from any other buildings, trees, or objects that might restrict the wind flow. These factors matter because the wind hitting the turbine needs to be steady and non-turbulent. As explained earlier, people who own a wind power system either are not happy with the system because it does not produce much, or they dislike where they live because it is too windy. Once again, having a small wind turbine on a sailboat seems to work the best.

Hybrid System

When considering a residential alternative energy system, combining wind and solar may have merit. According to the U.S. Department of Energy, "In much of the United States, wind speeds are low in the summer when the sun shines brightest and longest. The wind is strong in the winter when less sunlight is available. Because the peak operating times for wind and solar systems occur at different times of the day and year, hybrid systems are more likely to produce power when you need it." (Energy, 2023).

Conclusion

If the conditions are favorable for using wind power generation on a homestead, it would be a good complement to combine solar with the wind system, using the same batteries and inverter. There would be separate charge controllers for the solar and wind. These two modes of power generation could complement each other, with solar providing power in the day and wind generating at night.

References

Backwoods. (2022). *Backwoods Solar Catalog and Planning Guise, page 55*. Backwoods Solar.

Energy. (2023).
https://www.energy.gov/energysaver/hybrid-wind-and-solar-electric-systems

Chapter 9: Power Grid - Alternative Energy: Micro-Hydro

Some consider micro-hydro to be the most desirable option for alternative energy power generation. One reason is that if the water source is not seasonal but running continually year-round, it likely will work 24-7, providing dependable, continuous power for the property's needs. According to the Energy Saving Trust, "Whether it's from a small stream or a larger river, small or micro hydroelectricity systems, also called hydropower or hydro systems, can produce enough electricity for all electrical appliances and lighting in the average home." (EST, 2021). Unfortunately, most site locations do not have the needed features to make this option possible.

Head

There are two main topographies needed which are head and flow. Head is the vertical distance from the entry point of the intake pipe to the turbine in the powerhouse. The larger the head, the more pressure will be realized at the turbine. The U.S. Office of Energy Saver states that, "Most micro-hydropower sites are categorized as low or high head. The higher the head the better because you'll need less water to produce a given amount of power and you can use smaller, less expensive equipment. Low head refers to a change in elevation of less than 66 feet (20 meters)". (Energy, 2023).

To measure the head, a person could use the Google Earth app on a smartphone. At the top and bottom of the potential waterpipe, pinpoint the locations on the map. Each point will identify the elevation of that location at the bottom of the Google Earth window. By subtracting the small number from the large number, one can estimate the vertical elevation distance or head.

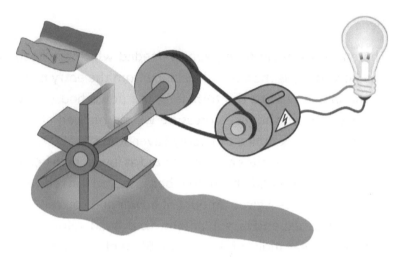

Micro-Hydro image source: Pixabay

Flow

The other topographic factor to consider is the amount of water available for use in the micro-hydro system. This is called flow, which is calculated by gallons per minute. A way to figure out the flow rate is to find a place in the stream where water drops such as the outflow of the culvert, or by creating a temporary dam and small waterfall. Then take a five-gallon bucket and a stopwatch to measure the gallons per minute.

"If your hydropower system will be producing electricity for a household, you will be most concerned with minimum flows. A good flow sampling through the dry season — assuming you know when the dry season is — will usually be adequate." (Kindberg, 2023).

Penstock

By establishing the head and flow, the calculations can be used to establish the potential for generating electricity from that stream. Water is collected at the intake in a small reservoir called a forebay. The water enters a pipe to carry the water down the hill to the powerhouse. This pipe is called a penstock.   As the water travels down the hill through the penstock, water pressure builds. The maximum pressure is at the bottom of the penstock as the water runs through the power generator.

High Head, Low-Pressure Turbines

There are different types of micro-hydro power generators depending on the amount of head and pressure. The system we have been talking about is a high-head, low-pressure application. This category of micro-hydro system will use one of three types of impulse turbines: Pelton Wheel, Crossflow, or Turgo turbines. Some comparative research should be done prior to selecting which turbine to use. They all operate on the principle of fast-flowing water from the penstock rushing through the turbine and then returning to the creek.

The University of Calgary's Energy Education website describes a Pelton Wheel turbine. "The Pelton turbine has a fairly simplistic design. A large circular disk is mounted on some sort of rotating shaft known as a rotor. Mounted on this circular disk are cup shaped blades known as buckets evenly spaced around the entire wheel. Then nozzles are arranged the wheel and serve the purpose of introducing water to the turbine. Jets of water emerge from these nozzles, tangential to the wheel of the turbine. This causes the turbine to spin as a result of the impact of the water jets on the buckets." (EE, 2023).

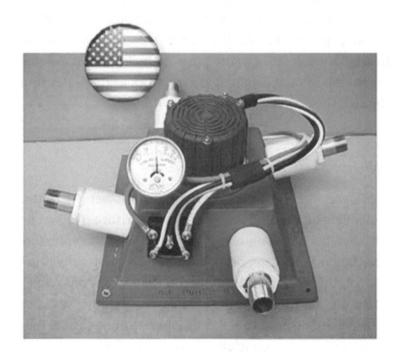

Micro-Hydro Power Generator used with permission from Backwoods Solar

Low-Head, Low-Pressure Turbines

Alternativeenergy.com explains, "For low-pressure low-head micro-hydro power schemes Reaction Turbines such as the *Francis, Kaplan* or *Crossflow turbines* are best suited. This is in part to the fact that the turbine blades of a reaction turbine are fully immersed in the waters flow." (AE, 2023).

Reaction Turbines can be used for low-head, low-pressure situations in that they use the velocity of moving water, such as a flowing river, to rotate blades that are in an enclosed case. These turbines are completely submersed in the river or creek, unlike the high-head, low-pressure units. If deciding to purchase one of these low-head, low-pressure turbine options, some comparative research should be done prior to selecting.

Water Rights and Regulations

Another important factor that needs to be considered is the water rights for that creek. Ideally, the intake of the pipe and bottom of the pipe at the powerhouse would be completely on the landowner's property. Some states allow micro-hydro power generation without any regulatory limitations, while others are very complicated. In areas where there are governing restrictions, different governing agencies need to sign off on the project to get a permit. This process can sometimes be lengthy, and any one agency could halt the process completely. These entities could include Native American tribes, national or state fish and wildlife government agencies, and county planning departments.

If the location has enough flow and head, and there are no limitations placed on building a micro-hydro system, then this can be a very desirable option.

References

EST. (2021, September 7). *Hydroelectricity.* https://energysavingtrust.org.uk/advice/hydroelectricity/

Energy. (2023). *Planning A Microhydropower system.* Energy.gov. https://www.energy.gov/energysaver/planning-microhydropower-system

Kindberg, L. (2023). *Micro-hydro power: A beginners guide to design and installation.* ATTRA. https://attra.ncat.org/publication/micro-hydro-power-a-beginners-guide-to-design-and-installation/

EE. (2023). *Pelton turbine.* Pelton turbine - Energy Education. https://energyeducation.ca/encyclopedia/Pelton_turbine

AE (2023). *Low Pressure Micro Hydro Power Plant Tutorial.* Alternative Energy Tutorials. https://www.alternative-energy-tutorials.com/hydro-energy/micro-hydro-power.html

Chapter 10: Power Grid - Alternative Energy: Geothermal

In this chapter, we will be looking at whether geothermal can be used for generating off-grid electrical power. "Geothermal energy is heat within the earth. The word geothermal comes from the Greek words geo (earth) and therme (heat). Geothermal energy is a renewable energy source because heat is continuously produced inside the earth. People use geothermal heat for bathing, for heating buildings, and for generating electricity...The slow decay of radioactive particles in the earth's core, a process that happens in all rocks, produces geothermal energy." (EIA, 2022). Yellowstone's Old Faithful Geyser is one famous example.

Yellowstone Old Faithful Geyser image source: Pixabay

Geothermal Case Study

Christopher Mims, in a 2008 Scientific American article stated that, "Today, 99 percent of Iceland's electricity is produced from renewable sources, 30 percent of which is geothermal (the rest is from dams—and there are a lot of them), according to Iceland's National Energy Authority. When transportation, heating and production of electricity are considered as a whole, geothermal provides half of all the primary energy used in Iceland." (Mims, 2008).

Since the hot water and steam are relatively near the earth's surface in that region, Iceland has been able to tap directly into this ever-available natural resource. They heat homes and other buildings by piping this hot water or steam throughout the area. Additionally, they can use steam to run turbines to generate electricity.

What About Where You Live?

Iceland's unique situation is not the typical case in most of the world. Unless you have a hot spring in your back yard, you will not have the option to heat your house completely from geothermal. But fortunately, geothermal technology can work in most any geographic location to reduce your heating and cooling costs.

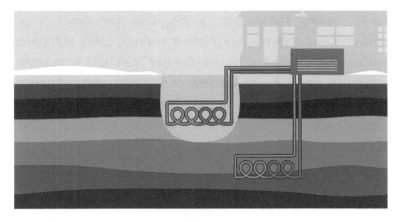

Geothermal Heat Pump image source: U.S. Department of Energy

Geothermal Heat Pumps

The U.S. Government claims that "Geothermal heat pumps use the constant underground temperatures of the shallow earth as thermal storage that enables efficient heating and cooling. Systems can vary in the type of collector and connections used." (Energy, 2023). Geothermal Heat Pumps (GHP) can be a viable option when building a house and can result in a short payback period due to substantially lower electric bills.

Savings

The U.S. Office of Energy Efficiency and Renewable Energy explains, "Although the purchase and installation cost of a residential GHP system is often higher than that of other heating and cooling systems, properly sized and installed

GHPs deliver more energy per unit consumed than conventional systems. For further savings, GHPs equipped with a device called a "desuperheater" can heat household water. In the summer cooling period, the heat removed from the house is used to heat the water for free. In the winter, water heating costs are reduced by about 50%." (EERE, 2023).

Heating a Greenhouse with Geothermal

An interesting innovation of how to use geothermal for heating is exemplified by the "Greenhouse in the Snow" project in snowy Alliance, Nebraska. A full explanation and interesting greenhouse video tour is available at their website: https://greenhouseinthesnow.com/. This area of Nebraska is famous for cold winters, dropping to 20 degrees F in the winters with a record low of 40 below zero. A retired mailman built his geothermal greenhouse over 30 years ago and has routinely grown lemons, limes, birds of paradise, hibiscus, and other tropical plants all year round! The greenhouse captures warm air from underground geothermal pipes and circulates that warm air through the greenhouse, resulting in no need for any other heat source, even in the winter. (GITS, 2019).

Geothermal Greenhouse image used with permission from
Greenhouse in the Snow

While these are examples of temperature-controlled
buildings with heat from underground, creating electricity
using geothermal is not very likely an option. That said,
electric bills can be reduced with a geothermal-equipped
forced air furnace in the home, while a greenhouse can be
temperature controlled with the only heat source being
geothermal.

Geothermal Greenhouse image used with permission from Greenhouse in the Snow

Enhanced Geothermal

On a larger scale, the United States government has been funding experimental projects to increase geothermal output by pressurizing the underground heat sources to make the heat more accessible for power generation above ground. These kinds of approaches, at this point, do not help the individual homeowner looking for ways to be off-grid or to generate residential electricity. But even though electrical power generating is generally not an option for making geothermal alternative power for home use, keep in mind the heat-saving options we have discussed and how it could then reduce one's monthly electric utility costs.

References

EIA. (2023, May 26). *U.S. Energy Information Administration - EIA - independent statistics and analysis*. Photovoltaics and electricity - U.S. Energy Information Administration (EIA). https://www.eia.gov/energyexplained/geothermal/

Mims, C. (2008, October 20). *One Hot Island: Iceland's Renewable Geothermal Power*. Scientific American. https://www.scientificamerican.com/article/iceland-geothermal-power/

EERE (2023). *Geothermal heat pumps*. Energy.gov. https://www.energy.gov/eere/geothermal/geothermal-heat-pumps

Energy. (2023). *Choosing and installing geothermal heat pumps*. Energy.gov. https://www.energy.gov/energysaver/choosing-and-installing-geothermal-heat-pumps

GITS. (2019). *Greenhouse in the snow*. https://greenhouseinthesnow.com

Chapter 11: Power Grid- Alternative Energy: Pedal Power

Possibly the least likely alternative energy option that is still worth discussing is using human muscle to generate electricity. While exercising is a good practice for healthy living, and doing it on a stationary bike has the potential to generate electricity, the question is how much electricity can be produced in a practical sense? It is possible that the amount of energy a person can generate exercising on a stationary bike, likely is not worth the effort for the little amount of power produced. An exception could be if the person would be using the stationary bike anyway as a form of a daily workout routine.

Pedal Power Potential

According to some, a typical household uses about 1000 kilowatt-hours of electrical power in a month. Is it possible to make enough electricity on a generator-equipped stationary bike to fulfill this need? Not even close. Adam Frank, a University of Rochester astrophysics professor explains it this way, "Pedaling a bike at a reasonable pace generates about 100 watts of power. That's the same energy-per-time used by a 100-watt lightbulb. So, if you pedaled eight hours every day for 30 days (no weekends off), then doing the math, you'd generate 24 kilowatt-hours (kWh) of energy...That's only 2.4 percent of the energy your house sucks up each month...Biking, full time, every day, no weekends, for four weeks gets you to just a few percent of your monthly energy use." (Frank, 2016).

An Intriguing Idea

Even though the benefits in terms of electrical power generated are dismal, a person might still be intrigued by the idea of converting muscle to electricity. For these individuals, there are two options. One is to buy a commercially built unit. Second, for those who are handy and like taking on interesting projects, build one yourself.

Pedal Power image used with permission from K-Tor, LLC

Commercially Available Power Bikes

One example of a commercially available exercise bike modification that can generate power is the "Pedal A Watt". This innovation is purchased ready-made to fit any bicycle. The back wheel of the bike is simply mounted onto the Pedal A Watt. The faster the cyclist pedals, the more power is made. It was used by someone on the Doomsday Prepper TV series produced by National Geographic.

Build Your Own Power Bike Projects

There have been several attempts by students in educational institutions to design and build a power-generating bike. One such school was the University of North Carolina, at Chapel Hill. In 2022, they uploaded to the Internet a PDF document of instructions showing pictures of the steps they took to create such a bike. The steps were: Obtain a bicycle and remove the back tire. Build a stand. Attach a motor to the stand. Connect with a drive belt. Place a diode in series with the motor and battery. (UNC, 2022).

Student-Built Pedal Power Bike

Another attempt by students to make a power bike was made by middle and high school-aged students at Flagstaff Junior Academy and Orme School in Northern Arizona. They worked on making a bike blender and a bike generator. With the help of grant funding, students were able to learn about step-by-step instructions and curriculum for other schools to use. This project was "a great tool for explaining difficult concepts like energy, power, electricity, and energy conversions. When students use the bike generator, they get a physical, hands-on understanding of these concepts." (NAU, 2018).

The practicality of making significant amounts of electrical power from a pedal bike is dismal, for those eager to try something innovative while burning off some calories, a pedal-powered generator may be worth considering. When considering human-powered electrical generating systems, one that seems to be very worthwhile and practical is an emergency radio that can be hand-cranked. A good example of this is an American Red Cross FRX3+ by Eton. Not only can you hand crank to keep the radio working when the batteries die, but it also has a USB port to be able to use the crank to be able to charge a cell phone or other small USB-charged device. This radio has many bands including AM/FM and all 7 NOAA and Environment Canada weather bands. It also includes an LED flashlight, alarm clock, and glow-in-the-dark indicator for an emergency. (Eton, 2023).

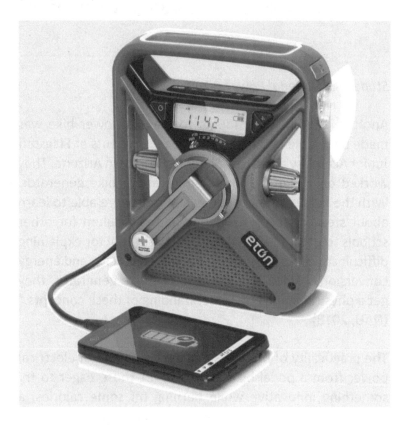

Crank-Powered Emergency Radio image source: American Red Cross

As you can see, there are some ways to generate electricity without natural resources such as the sun, wind, or flowing water. Pedal bikes may not make very much power but might be very important in an emergency. Even if a pedal bike would not be practical for your situation, a hand-cranked emergency radio would be highly recommended.

References

Frank, A. (2016, December 8). *Could you power your home with a bike?*. NPR. https://www.npr.org/sections/13.7/2016/12/08/504 790589/could-you-power-your-home-with-a-bike

University of North Carolina, at Chapel Hill. (2022, May). *Instructables.com - how to build a bicycle generator - Sustainable Carolina*. How to Build a Bicycle Generator. https://sustainable.unc.edu/wp-content/uploads/sites/257/2022/05/How-To-Build-A-Bicycle-Generator.pdf

Northern Arizona University. (2018, August). *Building a bike generator - Northern Arizona University*. Building a Bike Generator. https://in.nau.edu/wp-content/uploads/sites/156/2018/08/how-to-build-a-bike-generator-ek.pdf

Etón E-Commerce. (n.d.). *American Red Cross FRX3+ multi-powered Weather Alert Radio*. https://etoncorp.com/products/frx3

Chapter 12: Power Grid- Alternative Energy: Choices

Cost Effectiveness of Alternative Energy

One might question whether you save money choosing alternate energy. That depends on what incentives are available in your area and what your intentions are by going solar or other alternative energy methods. Depending on whether you are considering grid-tied or grid-backup or off-grid, it still takes a considerable amount of initial funds. Other factors to contemplate are whether you are planning to have a whole house system, and how many extreme cuts in your overall power needs you are willing to give up. We will now consider each of these options to have a better understanding of the cost of generating your own power.

Federal Tax Incentives

As explained earlier, at the time of the publishing of this book, there was at 30% energy efficiency federal tax credit available in the USA. This applies to any out-of-pocket expenses, whether you hire an installer or do it yourself.

Tax Credits

Tax credits reduce the amount of income tax you owe. For instance, if your total tax on your return is $2,000, but you are eligible for a $2,000 tax credit, then the amount owned drops to zero. Some homeowners might find a tax credit to not be a practical option because they are retired or on a fixed income. If you don't pay any income tax, then you can't benefit from the tax credit for energy efficiency.

Do Your Research

In past years the percentage of tax credit was lowered year after year, so research what the current percentage is at the time you build your system. Also, the out-of-pocket expenses documented for a given year may be a tax credit for that year. Any tax credit that would be left over may roll over to subsequent years.

State Tax Incentives

Any additional incentives available from the state in which you live will vary widely, so you will need to check that for your location. Some states have new incentives, such as Illinois, while other states are less or non-existent. Some reimbursements require the system to be professionally installed. Again, check for options available in your state.

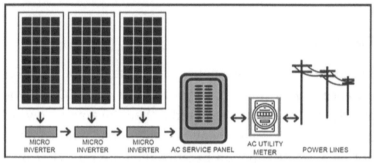

GRID TIE SYSTEM w/ MICROINVERTERS & WITHOUT BATTERIES

Grid-Tied Schematic image used with permission from Backwoods Solar

Grid-Tied

We will now compare grid-tied, grid-backup, and off-grid. Grid-tied systems are very popular because they allow for some form of major savings on the power bill each month. For instance, someone who just installed a grid-tied system paid all costs out of pocket. This system will pay for itself in about five years, with the federal tax credit and additional state incentives. Their power bill dropped from over $400 a month to just a minor fee of about $15. Others with only the federal tax credit, estimate eleven years to recover the costs.

Grid-Backup

A grid-backup approach is an option for an individual wanting to build a large solar system but not be officially connected to the grid. This approach still takes advantage of the federal tax credit for all parts and documented paid labor, but does not qualify to "sell back" to the power company. By choosing to not connect with a two-way meter, they do not have the option to have the system pay for itself except for the power savings. An advantage is that no outside agency would be involved. In this case, the power grid is used as a backup to the solar system. The inverter is set to use the solar during the day to power the house and charge the batteries. If the power generated does not keep up with the power needs, such as on a dark cloudy day in the winter, the inverter automatically would draw from the power grid to make up the difference.

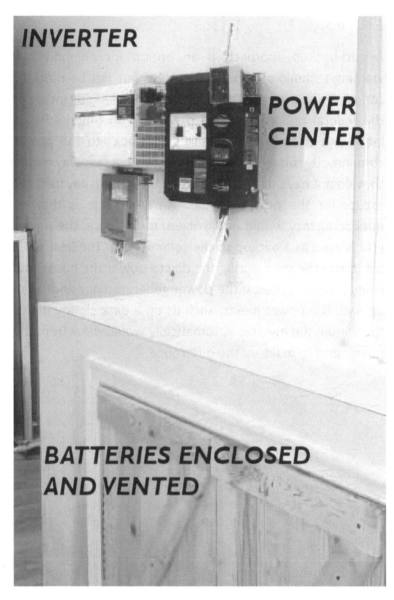

Off-Grid Power Room image used with permission from
Backwoods Solar

Off-Grid

For those individuals who want or need to have complete independence from the power company, being off-grid is the answer. This choice might even be the only option because the property is so remote that it is impossible or much too expensive to bring in power. In some areas, it costs about $10,000 per power pole to reach the property. An off-grid system may still qualify for the federal tax credits but not likely any state incentives. When completely off-grid, there would be the need to analyze one's electrical power needs very carefully. Often, those who are off-grid have learned to cut *way* back on electricity usage. For instance, anything that generates heat such as ovens, stoves, dryers, hot water tanks, and home heating would all need to be accomplished with some method other than electricity. This conversion is generally done with propane, except for heat which would likely be wood. Many off-grid homes even have propane refrigerators. Some kinds of electrical components such as ceiling fans may be 12-volt DC to save electricity.

Back-Up Generator

Some off-grid, grid-tied, or grid-backup systems may include a backup generator. This can be a portable generator, which might be 7 to 9 kilowatts in size or a full-house generator. These can be purchased to run on gas, propane, or diesel. Some are dual fuel. One individual had a portable generator that was dual fuel, which they ran on gas during the construction of their house. Then upon completion of the house, it was plumbed into propane permanently as the backup generator. Larger backup generators are capable of being automatically turned on and off by the inverter when needed. Others cannot and would require manually starting and stopping, as people do when there is a power failure during a storm.

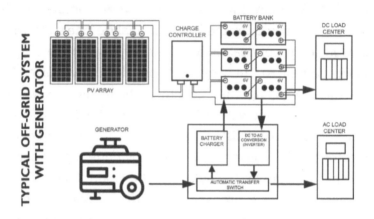

Off-Grid Schematic image used with permission from Backwoods Solar

Lead-Acid Batteries

Any of these alternative energy systems can utilize batteries to allow storage of power to be used later. For instance, solar would generate in the day and not at night. Batteries allow the house to be powered throughout the night. There are two common types of batteries: lead acid and lithium. Lead acid looks like car batteries but are deep-cycle such as the ones used in golf carts. While golf cart batteries can be used for alternative energy systems, there are more expensive ones that are specifically designed for alternative energy. Very large lead-acid batteries such as those used in forklifts can also be used. Historically, lead acid batteries cost less than lithium, although that may change as technology progresses. Lead-acid batteries are heavy and require monthly maintenance such as checking the depth of charge and topping off the water.

Lithium Batteries

The modern technology of batteries is lithium. These are the kind of batteries used in portable power tools and electric cars. Lithium batteries are more compact, lighter, and can be discharged deeper than lead-acid batteries. They require no maintenance. One disadvantage is that lithium batteries have been known to catch on fire.

Alternative Energy Options image source: Pixabay

Making a Choice

As you have seen, there are many options on how to generate electricity. A person planning for alternative energy should consider all of the pros and cons of each alternative energy system. This will allow the individual to make the best selection based on what resources are available on a particular property. The cost of installation and available natural resources should be taken into consideration. Remember, it is cheaper to cut back on electrical use than to generate that power.

The Cost of Energy Independence

"In remote locations, stand-alone systems can be more cost-effective than extending a power line to the electricity grid (the cost of which can range from $15,000 to $50,000 per mile). But these systems are also used by people who live near the grid and wish to obtain independence from the power provider or demonstrate a commitment to non-polluting energy sources." (Energy, 2023)

Solar Pros and Cons

The most popular form of alternative energy by far is solar. This is due to several factors. For one, there are no moving parts to maintain, as compared to wind or micro-hydro systems. A second benefit of solar is cost. Solar panel prices have dropped as well as becoming more efficient over the years. A disadvantage of solar is it only generates power in daylight, with no power whatsoever at night.

Solar Orientation

Does the location have adequate sun exposure or are there trees that could block the sun? What is the orientation of the property? For those living north of the equator, if the land is on the north side of a hill, then solar would not work efficiently, if at all. Therefore, while solar is often the best choice for an alternative energy system, it completely depends on the location of the panels, the amount of sun in the "solar window", as well as the orientation of the property to the sun.

Roof Mounted Panels

Another consideration with solar is where are the panels going to be installed. Basically, there are two options. First is on the roof of a building. Of course, this completely depends on whether the side of the roof faces south. Most people try to mount solar panels on the south-facing side of the house roof. On the other hand, I have a friend who has chosen to install a very large residential solar system, which he installed himself. He has panels on the south, west, and east sides of his roof. This way he captures the morning sun, then the middle of the day sun, and the afternoon sun in the west. It seems to work fine.

Ground Mounted Panels

The other mounting option is to mount the panels on a rack on the ground. One benefit of a ground-mounted system is it is easier and safer to install. No need to climb on a roof and run the risk of falling. Another advantage is that the rack can be oriented to take the best advantage of the sun's direction. Some people choose to use a pole with a set of solar panels on the pole with an automatic motor to rotate the panels during the day to be able to face the sun directly throughout the day, as it moves from east to west. There is a limit to how many panels can be mounted in this way. A pole-mounted system now has a moving part to maintain, so this could be a disadvantage. Since the price of solar panels has dropped so much, it is often thought a better choice to simply install more solar panels instead of using the pole mount approach.

Wind Pros and Cons

If a person lives in a windy geographic area, then wind power generation might be an option. It is often believed that a residential wind generator would require a minimum of 8 miles per hour of wind to even begin to make power. Added wind speed will result in an increase in the amount of power generated. When considering a wind turbine, keep in mind that the rating of the generator is based on the potential power. If it is rated to be full power at 15 miles per hour, then 8 miles an hour will be significantly less power generated.

The Need for Speed

Another consideration is how often it is windy. If wind is seasonal, with enough wind predominantly during half of the year, then the remainder of the year would not create enough electricity. Besides analyzing the seasonal winds, one needs to consider the daily patterns of wind. For instance, if the wind only comes up in the evenings, the rest of the 24 hours would not be generating significant power.

Disappointed with the Wind

An ideal place for a wind generator system might be on an oceanfront property or in a draw between two mountains. Some people say if you have a wind generator, you will either be frustrated with the wind because it is too much wind or upset at the windmill because it is not making enough power or is broken. For a wind system to work efficiently it needs to be high enough to not have obstructions from nearby objects such as buildings or trees. Consequently, most wind generators are mounted high up on a tower. This fact makes setting up and maintaining the system more difficult and possibly dangerous.

Windless

We have a family in our county that invested in a tower and wind generator, but unfortunately there never is enough wind. Also, in our area, there is a very large tower and a commercial size wind generator, but lately, the tower stands alone with no wind generator on top. In both cases, I must assume that either there was not enough wind to be practical for that location or it mechanically failed.

Crash and Burn

One other negative story about windmills is a friend of mine who owns solar panels plus a wind generator on a tower. The system was advertised to withstand high winds by automatically shutting off in a storm. Unfortunately, this was a false claim. Those who purchased this system damaged the generator motor during a storm because it did not shut down as advertised. To make matters worse, when my friend attempted to lower his tower, it fell the last part of the way down to the ground and broke the blades. Now the motor and the blades needed replacing. You can see that in a few instances, wind may be a good option, but in many cases, it is not the number one choice.

Micro-Hydro Pros and Cons

One alternative energy system that is a very good option is micro-hydro. The benefit is that it produces power all day and all night, assuming there is a continual, year-round flow of water. Like the wind option, one disadvantage is that it does have moving parts. But in this case, there is only one moving part, and that generator is designed to run continually. These systems require little to no maintenance for the most part. Unlike a large commercial hydroelectric dam, a micro-hydro system generates DC power which can then be stored for later use, and by using an inverter can supply typical household needs.

Falling Water

For those who are fortunate to have a steady flow of water on their property can capture the energy of falling water. The key factor to consider is how far the water drops before it gets to the generator. The vertical distance from the intake of the supply pipe and the drop of the pipe at the generator in the powerhouse needs to be high enough to make enough pressure to run the generator adequately. The more the drop or head, the more the generator will make electricity.

Different States, Different Rules

There is one last issue when considering micro-hydro for a power source is regulations. There are some areas of the USA where you can do what you want with the water on your land, allowing you the freedom to build a micro-hydro system on the property to provide the electrical needs for your house. However, other states do not allow micro-hydro installations without some complicated permitting processes. In these cases, it can involve multiple agencies, any one of which could negatively impact the project indefinitely.

Legal Limitations

Legal implications can impact the ability to install a micro-hydro system. These can include but are not limited to fish and wildlife regulations, tribal water rights, or a state's claims to being able to control water use. One example is a state that claimed a hundred or more years ago that all water in the state belonged to everyone, including creeks, lakes, underground aquifers, and rain coming out of the sky. Therefore, that state regulates all water usage, requiring permits for water usage, whether from a well, creek, or rain. Operating a micro-hydro system illegally in these areas could result in serious consequences. If you are fortunate enough to own land including a creek with enough vertical drop all year long, and no limiting regulations, then building a micro-hydro system would be ideal.

Geothermal Pros and Cons

Geothermal utilizes the contrast in temperature between underground and above ground. The most common geothermal approach is in connection with an electric heating and air conditioning system. I have two friends who have dug trenches in their home's fields, installed piping underground (often eight feet down) and pumped fluid through the pipes to be utilized at the house. In these two cases, people installed an electric heat pump system at their houses instead of the typical outdoor heat exchanger unit. They use the difference in the temperature of the underground and ambient air temperature to accomplish the same job done by a conventional heat pump. The result is using much less electricity to heat the house as compared to an older heating system. The side benefit of either heat pump method is to gain the extra perk of having air conditioning. From an alternative energy point of view, the disadvantage of a geothermal heat pump system is that the system still uses electricity so is not a source for generating electricity off-grid.

Pedal Power Pros and Cons

There are commercial and homemade pedal bikes that are connected to an electrical generator that produces power whenever someone is pedaling that stationary bike. While this can be a fun novelty and does create electricity, it does not generate nearly enough power to serve an entire house. It probably only makes enough for a small device like powering a laptop. So, from a practical vantage point, a pedal power generator is not very useful. To make matters worse, it only works when someone is sweating! No effort in – no power out.

Wood Gasification Pros and Cons

There is a somewhat experimental method of creating electricity worth mentioning in passing. Wood gasification is a process of burning firewood and capturing a fuel byproduct that can be used to run a generator to make electricity. While this can be a fun experimental project, it ultimately requires a constant supply of firewood and someone to keep feeding the fire with wood, to make a comparatively small amount of fuel for the generator. It is therefore the opinion of this author that wood gasification is not to be taken seriously as an option for alternative power generation.

Gas Generator Pros and Cons

Most people who live off-grid will have one or more of the above-mentioned methods of creating electricity to supply their homestead. For instance, they might have solar and wind. This allows the potential of capturing the sun during the day and maybe the wind at night. Having more than one system working together is called a "hybrid" system. In any case, most off-grid homes also have a gas generator as a backup. This helps in the winter when the limited sun does not supply enough power from the solar panels, for instance. Having a backup generator is a very good idea.

There are basically three fuel options for a power generator: gasoline, propane, and diesel. While many of these fuel options are viable choices, propane seems to be the preferred option. This may be because propane has an unlimited shelf life. In other words, propane won't degrade or lose its potency. Gasoline stays fresh for about a few months and then starts to deteriorate. Diesel lasts longer but not indefinitely.

Consequently, most off-grid homes utilize a propane backup generator to fill the power void. It is worth noting that some portable generators are dual fuel, meaning they can operate on more than one type of fuel, such as gas or propane. One more thing to know about backup generators is that the better ones include an auto-start option so when the batteries of the alternative energy system run low, the inverter automatically starts the generator to charge up the batteries and/or provide the power needed for the house.

References

Energy. (2023). *Off-grid or stand-alone Renewable Energy Systems*. Energy.gov. https://www.energy.gov/energysaver/grid-or-stand-alone-renewable-energy-systems

Additional Video and Podcast Resources

www.preparingforthetimeoftrouble.com - Part 36 "Alternative Energy: Solar Power Systems Tour"

Chapter 13: Water Grid – Safe Water Sources

As stated earlier, the three most important things to staying alive is air, water, and food. A person can live about three days without water; therefore, the most important feature of a potential country property is water. Air is abundant on any property, though some air quality might be better than others. Food can be grown in almost any location if the needed amendments are brought into the location to grow plants productively.

Water Availability

Water is a natural resource that can't be found everywhere and cannot be delivered to a property cost-effectively. Consequently, the number one feature of looking for land is the availability of a water source. Water on the homestead is needed for drinking, domestic use, and irrigation. A person might be excited to find a seemingly perfect parcel of land, with southern exposure for solar power generation and abundant sunlight for growing gardens. It may even have a picturesque or panoramic view, but if there is no water source then the property is not suitable for developing a country homestead.

Water Sources

Water sources can come in different forms. Typically, water is extracted from a water table underground with the use of a well. Water can also be found by developing a spring discovered on the property. City water sources are generally collected from rivers or natural lakes otherwise surface water is routed into large reservoirs. On islands or in arid areas, rainwater harvesting is sometimes an option for an individual's property. We will now examine each of these four sources of water.

Hand-Dug Water Well image source: U.S. Farm Security Administration

Hand-Dug Wells

According to the U.S. Geological Survey, there are four main types of wells. The first is a hand-dug well, which is a hole in the ground dug by hand or by some other form of digging. It is typically a large enough hole to climb in. These are the kinds of wells used in historic times. Jacob's Well, in the Bible, is a good example. (John 4:6). According to Mariam Berge, "Jacob's Well is holy in Christian, Jewish, Muslim, and Samaritan teachings. Tradition says it is where Jacob once camped 4,000 years ago, and where Jesus also passed through, holding a conversation with a Samaritan woman." (Berge, 2021). Even though this well was dug by hand it provided water by pulling the water bucket up to the surface with a rope.

Driven Well

The second type of well is a driven well, which is built by driving a small pipe into soft or sandy soil. The bottom of the pipe is screened to filter out particles. The weakness of this approach is that is cannot be driven through rock plus cannot go very deep. If the water table is shallow, it may be unusable or possibly dry up during summer.

Drilled Well

The third method is drilling a well. This method is how most modern wells are acquired. Large, expensive equipment is needed for this method and can drill hundreds or a thousand feet to locate water. Incorporating a continuous casing with this method results in having the least risk of contamination compared to hand-dug or driven wells.

Key Components

A drilled well is very common in country property and requires the use of several key components. The well uses a casing to prevents the hole from collapsing and keeps contaminants from entering the water supply. On the top of the well casing is a cap to keep insects and other unwanted contaminates from infiltrating the extracted water. The bottom of the well is protected with a screen to keep the pipe clear for a dependable flow of water. A pitless adaptor is a device to keep the water at the top of the well from freezing. Lastly, there is a pump in the casing which is submersible, meaning it is entirely in the water. (EPA, 2019).

Springs

Besides a typical well, a less common but equally viable option for a water source is a spring. All wells are an attempt to access water that is underground. A spring on the other hand is water that has found its way to the surface of the ground without human involvement. Springs, once again, have a very long history of being a source of water. In Bible times, springs provided water when the Israelites inherited the land of Canaan. (Deuteronomy 8:7). God had even previously provided water from springs from the rocks in the desert. As you can see, springs have been around for a long time as a source of water. The problem is they are rare.

We will discuss later a method to develop a trickle of water coming from the ground into a viable spring. There have been many cities down through history to the present day where there has been an artesian spring, pumping water out of the ground without the need for drilling or mechanical pumping. There is a city that has a pipe in the middle of town with perfect water that has run continually, day and night, for years and years. Drinkable water is free for the taking!

Surface Water

If you find a potential country property with a year-round creek, this is a very desirable and hard-to-find feature. While local regulations may restrict the ability to take water from the creek for personal use, this could at least be an option in case of an emergency source of water. Lakes and ponds are also an option. Some believe that water taken from the middle of a lake is purer than that removed from a stream. Even though municipalities often have a river, lake, or reservoir as the source of water, it requires significant water treatment to make it safe to drink. This is one reason why city water often has additives such as chlorine. Consequently, a private land owner may be limited by local regulations as to being able to depend on a creek, river, or lake for a primary source of domestic water.

Rainwater Catchment

Texas A & M AgriLife Extension explains, "Rainwater harvesting is an innovative alternative water supply approach anyone can use. Rainwater harvesting captures, diverts, and stores rainwater for later use. Implementing rainwater harvesting is beneficial because it reduces demand on existing water supply, and reduces run-off, erosion, and contamination of surface water." (TX A&M, 2023). Rain harvesting can be done on a small scale for irrigating gardens, or whole house systems to provide drinking or household use. Depending on rainwater catchment as a primary water source is often done on islands, and in areas where well drilling is unproductive or prohibited.

Water Purification

No matter which source of water one uses, that water needs to be tested. Drinking and domestic water likely would require filtration and water treatment such as using ultraviolet. Therefore, water testing is needed to establish which method of treatment would be required.

Water Sources

The following chapters will address in more depth each of these different sources of water for a person's country property. Water is vital for life and for developing a homestead. It is very important to consider carefully what source of water would be planned when purchasing land for a country home.

References

Berger, M. (2021, July 5). *Jacob's well: Meet the priest who protects this biblical sanctuary in the heart of the holy land*. The National. https://www.thenationalnews.com/world/mena/jacob-s-well-meet-the-priest-who-protects-this-biblical-sanctuary-in-the-heart-of-the-holy-land-1.818694

Environmental Protection Agency. (2019, November 6). *Learn about private water wells*. EPA. https://19january2021snapshot.epa.gov/privatewells/learn-about-private-water-wells_.html

Texas A & M AgriLife Extension. (2023). Rainwater harvesting. https://rainwaterharvesting.tamu.edu/rainwater-basics/

Chapter 14: Water Grid – Wells

While there are hand-dug wells, driven wells, and drilled wells, by far the most common well for developing new property is a drilled well. As explained by the U.S. Environmental Protection Agency, "Drilled wells are constructed by percussion or rotary-drilling machines. Drilled wells can be thousands of feet deep and require the installation of casing. Drilled wells have a lower risk of contamination due to their depth and use of continuous casing." (EPA, 2019).

Hand-Dug Well image source: Pixabay

Well Yield

A drilled well may hit a water table, but the amount of water flow is very important. This is measured by gallons per minute. Alabama Cooperative Extension System explains, "Wells completed in more porous, saturated geologic materials routinely result in high-yielding wells. Wells completed in less porous clays and bedrock can have slow groundwater yields, as slow as less than 5 gallons per minute." (ACES, 2023).

Well Logs

The problem with establishing if an undeveloped property has usable water from a well is somewhat guesswork. A very good first step is to look at recorded well logs, which are usually available at the county offices. By looking at the nearby properties' records one can establish a rough idea of how successful the neighboring wells have been. These well logs will show how deep each well is and possibly the gallons per minute yield. It is likely that the well logs would not reveal how good the water tastes or any contaminations.

Research Neighboring Wells

At that point, it would be a good idea to talk to each neighbor about their water. For instance, I know of a property where the nearby property had perfect water without a very deep well. The well driller said he hit a mountain aquafer. When that water was tested it did not even need filtering or UV treatment. On the other hand, the immediate neighboring five-acre property had arsenic in the water and was undrinkable. That well owner had been using the well water but buying drinking water. Another neighbor was unable to locate any water, while a different neighbor down the road would run out of water during a dry summer.

Taste and See

You can see that well logs and talking to neighbors about their water can be very helpful in trying to get an idea of the possibility of drilling a well. One more thing, if a neighbor claims that have perfect water, ask to taste the water. This can be revealing. One country home had so much iron in their well water that plumbing fixtures would get difficult, rust-colored stains. Can you imagine what that would do to your white clothes in the wash? A well with iron can be treated with filters and iron removal systems. This requires additional maintenance.

Water Dowsing

Most local well drillers are experienced enough to make an educated guess as to how deep they might have to drill to reach water and what the yield might be. Some might choose to use a water dowser. While there are people who fear that his approach is demonic in nature and should be avoided, others consider it is a geophysical phenomenon. Not everyone has the electrical makeup in their body to be able to do dowsing, but those who can are able to take two willow sticks or two L-shaped steel rods for the task. The person holds one stick or rod in each hand, and as they walk over an area with underground flowing water, the rods will cross, or the willow branch will bend down. Some have seen this work over a known underground water pipe. One dowser had the downward pull so hard that it would peel the bark of the willow branch.

Finding Water

The U.S. Geological Survey sees dowsing this way, "The natural explanation of 'successful' water dowsing is that in many areas underground water is so prevalent close to the land surface that it would be hard to drill a well and not find water. In a region of adequate rainfall and favorable geology, it is difficult not to drill and find water!" (USGS, 2018). It would be up to the potential land owner to decide, based on the research of neighboring well logs and the opinion of a trusted local well driller whether to gamble the funds to drill a well, considering the risks and the expense of the process.

Important Decisions

The next decision is whether to purchase the land, prior to drilling a well and just hope for the best or to make a successful well drilling effort be a contingency for the purchase of the land. In that case, the potential owner would be funding the well drilling operation. If successful, the land purchase transaction would be completed. If the well was dry, then the deal would be cancelled. The potential purchaser would have lost a great deal of money from the expense of drilling. At least one would not end up owning a property that now could not get a building permit due to having no viable well.

Community Wells

One option that might be available is the possibility of connecting to a community well. In this case, the neighboring property owners jointly have the rights to a larger well that is already in operation. The new landowner would join the community well association and then have the right to access water from that system. Taking advantage of a community well has the benefit of no large initial investment or risk but brings with it a relationship with the neighborhood water district, as some may call it. If a person wants to be totally off the "water grid", this option is still not completely self-sufficient.

Water Quality

As explained by the Water-Right Group, "Some people are under the impression that well water is "pure" since it comes from within the earth. However, it's rainwater that has moved through the air, across the ground, and through the soil. By the time well water gets into your home, there's likely more to it than just water. Those elements can affect your pipes, clothes, food, skin, and your health." (WRG, 2022).

Well Contamination

The National Ground Water Association says, "A well can easily be contaminated if it is not properly constructed or if toxic materials are released into the well. Toxic material spilled or dumped near a well can leach into the aquifer and contaminate the groundwater drawn from that well. Contaminated wells used for drinking water are especially dangerous. Wells can be tested to see what chemicals, pathogens and other contaminants may be in the well and if they are present in dangerous quantities." (NGWA, 2022). No matter which source of water you may use well, spring, creek, or rainwater, testing of the water may reveal the need for some form of treatment. This we will discuss in a future chapter.

References

Environmental Protection Agency. (2019, November 6). *Learn about private water wells*. EPA. https://19january2021snapshot.epa.gov/privatewell s/learn-about-private-water-wells_.html

Alabama Cooperative Extension System. 2023). *Problems with water yield in private water wells*. Alabama Cooperative Extension System. https://www.aces.edu/blog/topics/fish-water/problems-with-water-yield-in-private-water-wells/

USGS. (2018). *Water dowsing completed*. Water Dowsing | U.S. Geological Survey.

https://www.usgs.gov/special-topics/water-science-school/science/water-dowsing

National Ground Water Association. (2022, October 7). *Well basics - what is a well? - well water testing.* The Groundwater Foundation. https://groundwater.org/wells/

Water-Right Group. (2022, November 10). *How does a well work?: Water-right.* Water. https://www.water-right.com/homeowner-resources/how-does-a-well-work/

Additional Video and Podcast Resources

www.preparingforthetimeoftrouble.com - Part 190 "Water Wells on Country Property"

Chapter 15: Water Grid – Springs

Springs occur when underground water finds its way to the surface of the land without any mechanical pumping or human intervention. Some springs are concentrated in a small area and can produce a fair amount of water, while another type of spring is over a larger area of damp ground. To make a spring useful there is usually the need to develop the spring, which means improving the ability to capture and retain the water. Developing the spring also increases the chances of the resulting water being free from contaminants. A developed spring is usually housed in some form of protecting enclosure to keep animals and falling leaves from compromising the collected spring water.

Water Spring image source: Pixabay

Types of Springs

Penn State Extension explains it this way, "A spring is formed when natural pressure forces groundwater above the land surface. This can occur at a distinct point or over a large seepage area. Springs are sometimes used as water supplies and can be a reliable and relatively inexpensive source of drinking water if they are developed and maintained properly." PSE, 2023). If local regulations allow a spring to be a primary source of water, it is a wonderful option if the spring provides enough volume of water and does so year-round. If the water flow seeping out of the ground is enough volume and it is consistent, it is called a spring.

Hot Springs

When a person hears the term "spring", an image of a spring of cold water comes to mind. But there are springs with hot water. Hot springs are the result of the underground water being super-heated by rocks deep in the ground in a process called geothermal. Some locations on Earth provide enough geothermal-heated water or steam that can be used to heat buildings or even generate electricity. Some of these rare locations include Northern California, and countries like New Zealand, Iceland, and Italy.

Geothermal

Sometimes geothermal is generated in connection with a volcanic area resulting in a geyser. Old Faithful Geyser in Yellowstone National Park is an example of geothermal action due to volcanic activity. The United States National Park Service explains how a hot spring is formed, "In non-volcanic areas, the temperature of rocks within the Earth also increases with depth—this temperature increase is known as the Geothermal Gradient. If water percolates deeply enough into the crust, it comes into contact with hot rocks and can circulate to the surface to form hot springs." (NPS, 2020).

Commercial Hot Springs

Commercial hot springs are very popular for tourists. They can be enjoyable and therapeutic. Sometimes hot springs are available in a natural setting and do not need to add cold water to make it comfortable. These are usually small, such as the size of a hot tub, and may require hiking to a remote location to access. Commercially developed hot springs sometimes have more than one pool, with differing temperatures, allowing the swimmer to select the heat level to their liking. Some people start with a warm pool, then as their body climatizes, they move to hotter and hotter pools.

El Dorado Hot Springs image source: Library of Congress

Health Benefits of Hot Springs

According to freelance writer Vanessa Locampo, "Hot springs have been favored by various societies throughout history. Today, they are often used for relaxation and recreation, but evidence suggests that hot springs also provide a few health benefits to those who soak in them." She goes on to list several health benefits of soaking in these mineral hot springs: rehabilitation, painkilling properties, skin benefits, improving mental health, and even relief for chronic health conditions such as rheumatoid arthritis. (Locampo, 2023).

Roadside Springs

Sometimes a person may find a city with a spring or a roadside spring, where free water can be gathered and used for any purpose including drinking. While this might seem like a windfall, some cautions might need to be considered. The New York State Department of Health offers this advice, "Some communities have a local spring that residents use to collect water for drinking, cooking, and other household purposes. Springs occur where underground water comes out near the ground surface. Although the water may look pure and clean, it might not be. Often it is unknown what the source of the water is, or where it has traveled before being collected. A spring might flow above ground, allowing animal waste or chemicals to run into the water...Roadside springs are generally not protected from contamination and are not routinely tested." (NYSDH, 2023).

Gravity-Fed Springs

Most people will never find country property available to buy with a natural hot spring but will need to visit a commercial hot spring to enjoy these health benefits. A person might be fortunate enough to find land with a natural cold-water spring that can be developed. There is one country property with a spring that ran year-round and was up a hill from the house. This made it possible to have gravity-pressurized running water for household use. Consequently, this home did not need electricity to pump the water source from underground such as in the case of a well and did not need electricity to develop water pressure at the house. This is a very rare but ideal arrangement for a homestead water supply.

Spring Water Storage Cistern image source: Pixabay

Locating a Spring

Usually, when a person locates a potential spring on the property, it is not adequate in its natural state to provide all of the household needs. But many times, a seemingly unpromising spring can be developed to become useful, providing a consistent, reliable source of water for the family. This requires a sequence of steps to accomplish this development project.

Locating the Source

After locating a wet or seeping area on a hill on the property, the source of the spring will need to be located. This is done by digging into the hill and following the water. Hopefully, the source can be established. A few feet away from the spring source there would need to be a way to hold back the gravel which will be added.

Intake Area

This 4-foot-high wall can be compacted soil or concrete. Through this wall would be a pipe with a perforated section of pipe on the spring side of the wall. Drain rock gravel would be used to fill the hole up to the top of the wall.

Protective Covering

This creates an intake area for the water to collect and make its way into the pipe. This cavity would then be covered on the top to keep dirt from falling into the hole. This could be heavy Visqueen plastic sheeting. The remaining area above this would be filled with dirt up to ground level. Now the spring source is completely covered.

Piping

The pipe coming out of the cutoff wall would now carry the water to the spring box, which is likely a concrete tank designed to allow the water to settle the dirt and sand. The pipe carrying the good water away from the spring box is halfway between the bottom of the tank and the top of the water level. This ensures the carrying away of the cleanest water possible. A person may even wish to add a second tank as a cistern to hold the usable water, though this is not always required. After all this work, a person might become discouraged with how little water might be trickling out of the pipe, but the fact is a slow steady trickle, 24/7 can result in a significant amount of water.

Potential of a Spring

Most country properties will not have the potential of a spring, but it is worth investigating all corners of the property, especially on the uphill side, for any wet areas as compared to the rest of the ground. Searching for a spring should not be done on a rainy day! Finding and developing a usable spring is a very exciting and inexpensive possibility for any country property.

References

PSE. (2023). *Spring Development and protection.*
PennState Extension.
https://extension.psu.edu/spring-development-and-protection

NPS. (2020). *Hot springs/geothermal features.* National
Parks Service.
https://www.nps.gov/subjects/geology/hot-springs.htm

Locampo, V. (2023, February 24). *7 health benefits of Hot
Springs.* Hot Springs. https://hotsprings.co/health-benefits-of-hot-springs/

NYSDH. (2023). *Department of Health.* Don't Drink Water
from Roadside Springs.
https://www.health.ny.gov/environmental/water/drinking/springs.htm

USDA. (2009, January). Spring Development.
https://www.nrcs.usda.gov/sites/default/files/2022-09/stelprdb1167476-spring-development.pdf

Chapter 16: Water Grid – Rainwater Harvesting

"Harvesting rain is a practice that has been around for centuries. Cisterns and other rain harvesting systems are used globally and are commonplace. Benefits of collected rainwater include eliminating constraints due to restrictions on municipal water, reducing dependency and cost of locally supplied water, and providing a secure and dependable water source free of chemical treatment." (RainHarvest, 2023).

Rain Harvesting

One of the less commonly used sources for domestic and drinking water is rainwater harvesting, or rainwater catchment as it is sometimes called. While this approach is rare, it is more common on islands or other geographic areas where drilling a well for fresh water may not be possible. Amazingly, rainwater catchment has even been used in geographic regions with very little rainfall per year.

Rainwater Uses

RainHarvest Systems further explains, "Collected water can be used for outside applications such as irrigation and washing cars, and indoor uses such as flushing toilets and washing clothes to mention a few. Rainwater can be purified to use for bathing or as everyday drinking water. Rain harvesting is a great solution for off-grid living, and for many who depend solely on rain for day-to-day life." (RainHarvest, 2023).

While some governing agencies frown on or prohibit collecting water, some places like Austin, Texas encourage it with education programs, incentives, and tax breaks. According to Innovative Water Solutions, Austin is the nation's leading city to encourage rainwater harvesting and has the longest-running tax rebates. Rainwater catchment equipment and supplies are sales tax exempt. (Maxwell, 2023).

Incentives

Even at the state level in 2011, Texas House Bill 3391 was passed to encourage saving rainwater. John Kight is considered to be the guru of rainwater catchment. "One of the most important things the bill does, according to Kight, is changing the Texas Commission on Environmental Quality (TCEQ) rules on rainwater harvesting to encourage new state government buildings to have rainwater catchment systems for non-potable uses. Kight is also glad to see that the bill encourages financial institutions to make loans for homes, businesses, and developments that will use harvested rainwater as the sole source of water supply." (HCA, 2011).

Moratorium Against Harvesting Rainwater

There was an instance in Washington State where rainwater collection was not allowed for domestic use. A lawsuit over tribal water rights resulted in a moratorium of well drilling. This affected a very large geographic area, resulting in no longer allowing country property to be developed. Building permits require an approved source of water. This moratorium on new wells created a great problem. In that case, the Washington State Department of Ecology allowed those affected areas to utilize rainwater collection in lieu of drilling a well.

Due Diligence

Allowances and preventative regulations vary from state to state and county to county. A person looking for country property to develop should research this issue carefully, to make sure that the property can be allowed access to water through drilling a well or rainwater collection.

Residential Rain Barrels

A minor but common method of collecting rainwater is for irrigating plants. This small-scale application is relatively simple to set up and is quite inexpensive. The Environmental Protection Agency states that "Residential rain barrels are an inexpensive and easy retrofit that reduces stormwater runoff and provides irrigation water." (EPA, 2008).

Whole-House Rainwater Collection System

Some of the common uses for collecting rainwater are for drinking water and domestic uses, irrigation, providing water for livestock, and a resource for fire protection. The main components of a whole-house rainwater collection system starts with a rain collection area. This is usually the roofs of buildings but could include runoff collected into ponds. Next, the collected water must be routed to the storage location. Typically, this would be underground water piping that collects the various collection points into one larger pipe which then carries the water to storage tanks, called cisterns. These tanks are lower than the collection areas, so gravity carries the water without the need for a pump. Tanks can be outdoors above ground, in a tank shed, or underground.

Pros and Cons

Rainwater in and of itself is distilled water, free of some contaminants sometimes encountered in well water, such as iron or arsenic. On the other hand, collecting water on roofs has some potential for different types of issues. If the location is near salt water as in the case of an island, then it might be common for seagulls to perch on top of the roof, leaving their deposits. Also, if there are trees nearby, wind blowing might result in leaves, needles, or pollen landing on the roofs. For these reasons, it is necessary to take some precautions when collecting rainwater.

Preventative Measures

There are two main safeguards that should be incorporated into the collection system prior to being stored. The first is to screen out particulates from making their way into the storage tanks. This can be done with either a screen on the downspouts or in the rain gutters. Some may choose to use both, but in either case, these screens will need occasional inspection and cleaning of debris.

First Flush Diverter

The second device incorporated into the system to limit contaminants is called a first flush diverter. There are several designs for these, so some homework might be useful if planning a system. One such approach is the first flush diverter on each downspout. The other approach is having all downspout pipes making their way into one large diverter. Either way, the idea is that after a stretch of dry weather, the initial burst of water collected would be rerouted away as wastewater and dumped on the ground. Once that early dusty water is diverted, the remaining water from then on is sent to the cisterns for use.

Water Storage

The next section of a rainwater catchment system is the storage tanks or cisterns. If multiple tanks are used, then the incoming water pipe could be routed to the first tank, then daisy-chained in sequence from tank to tank. These would ultimately end up being connected to the tank from which the water would make its way to the house by way of a pump. The advantage of this configuration is that any dusty sediment that might still be in the water coming in, will settle to the bottom of the first tank. The outflow pipe taking the water to the next tank is several inches from the bottom, keeping the sediment below the outflow pipe level. It can also be incorporated into the first tank overflow outlet to prevent the incoming water from filling the tank too full. By installing an overflow outlet pipe, any excess water will be automatically sent from the tank to be disposed of on the ground away from the tank.

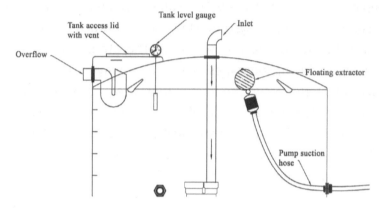

Rainwater Storage Tank image used with permission from RainHarvest Systems

You will notice in the illustration above, that in this case, the incoming water is directed through a pipe inside the tank to near the bottom and routed to discharge upward. This prevents the incoming water from stirring up the sediment and making the water murky.

While the above picture shows the overflow water being collected from the bottom, some collect from the top. In this case, a precautionary option is that some include a scoop-shaped end to the overflow pipe on the inside of the tank. This device, sometimes called a skimmer, works in such a way so that any debris floating on the top of the water in the first tank would be floated over the skimmer and out with the discharge. This approach would minimize any remaining floating debris from remaining in the tank.

Complete System

For a simpler system, below is a picture of a preconfigured RainFlo system available from RainHarvest Systems.

Rainwater Catchment System image used with permission from RainHarvest Systems

Whether you choose to collect water in rain barrels for small-scale irrigation of your landscaping or opt for a large-scale rainwater catchment system to provide the water needs of your country property, rainwater is a source of water directly from the sky. Rainwater is a clean water source and can be stored for year-round availability. While more expensive to set up and maintain than a well, a particular country property may have no other option for a source of water than rain harvesting.

References:

RainHarvest. (2023). *Rainwater Collection and Stormwater Management*. RainHarvest Systems LLC. https://www.rainharvest.com/shop/

Maxwell-Gaines, C. (2023, August 2). *Texas rainwater harvesting rebates and water conservation incentives*. Innovative Water Solutions LLC. https://www.watercache.com/rebates

HCA. (2011). *Education conservation cooperation - hillcountryalliance.org*. Hill Country Alliance. https://www.hillcountryalliance.org/uploads/HCA/News052411b.pdf

EPA. (2008). *U.S. Environmental Protection Agency | US EPA*. Managing Wet Weather with Green Infrastructure. https://www.epa.gov/sites/default/files/2015-10/documents/gi_munichandbook_harvesting.pdf

Chapter 17: Water Grid – Surface Water

Most country property owners find water sources by a well, a developed spring, or rainwater harvesting. Another possibility is surface water on the property. This can be a creek, river, pond, or lake. Most of the time this is not a practical way to gather water for domestic needs, because it is not safe, seasonally unreliable, or not allowed for this purpose due to government regulations.

Surface Water image source: Pixabay

Water Sources Were Once Rain

Flowing streams of water and standing water were originally the result of some form of precipitation draining into these waterways. Therefore, all water sources were originally moisture from the sky. Even underground sources were once rainwater that made its way into the earth. The process of moving around in underground aquafers usually helps purify the quality of the water or on rare occasions leaches contaminants into the water. This is why water testing is important if opting to use any water source for domestic use, especially drinking water.

Water Usage Restrictions

Some states do not restrict the use of water sources, while others are very controlling. One state, for instance, believed that all water was for the benefit of everyone, so in the early 1900s regulations were established for state control of all water resources in that state, whether underground, rainwater, or surface water. A state with little or no regulations makes it possible for a developer of country property to use any water resource on that property. When considering a location with the freedom to use water at will, a spring-fed stream or creek would be very beneficial. Those regions with strict policies will restrict or completely prohibit taking advantage of the surface water.

Ram Pumps

If a person owned land in an area with no restrictions, the ideal would be a healthy stream flowing downhill for some distance on that property. The elevation difference from top to bottom, or head, may be high enough that a person can use the force of the water to pump water uphill. For example, if a water pipe carries water downhill with a head of 100 vertical feet in a 2" pipe, this would create a great deal of pressure coming out of the pipe at the bottom. In this scenario, one could run that pipe into a ram pump. This type of pump, sometimes known as an impulse pump, takes the energy of falling water to push a smaller amount of water uphill.

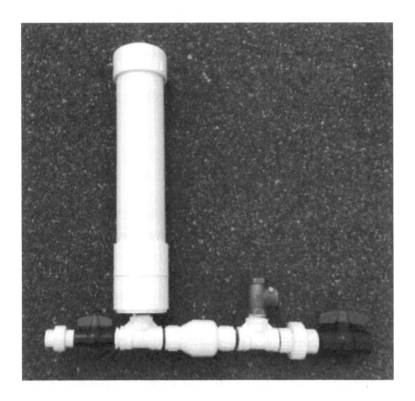

Ram Pump image used with permission from Land to House

This pump technology has been around for over a hundred years in America, used by farmers to provide water for livestock in an upper field. A ram pump does not require electricity but uses 90% of the water's energy to power the pump while sending 10% of the water uphill in a smaller pipe. Depending on the height of the head, this method can pump water much higher than the height of the original intake at the water source. Ram pumps only have two moving parts, so they are very dependable and capable of

159

running for years. Ram pumps can be purchased as a unit or can be built yourself using step-by-step instructions and YouTube video tutorials. An example of this is an article, "How to Build a Ram Pump" by florekel9521. (Instructables, 2023).

Hydro-Electric Power Generation

Another possible use for country property that has downhill flowing water is to generate electricity using a micro-hydro system. Like the above example of a ram pump, the effectiveness and output potential are dictated by the head, or vertical height from intake to the micro-hydro. The more head and the bigger the pipe, the more the electrical power generating potential. Once again, unless this project was done "in Cognito", the permitting process can be complicated and time-consuming, except for the states that has no regulations for the use of surface water for generating electricity.

Emergency Drinking Water

A very important benefit of having surface water on your property is for emergencies. One kind of emergency might be not having available water during difficult times or times of national emergency such as the power grid being down. Having a source of surface water would then be very helpful. It can even be life-saving to have some surface water such as a creek on the property. At least you could take a bucket to the creek and get some water. In this scenario, it would have been good to plan to already have on hand some form of water filtering equipment such as you might have for camping.

Filtering Water

The National Park Service advises, "Never drink water from a natural source that you haven't purified, even if the water looks clean. Water in a stream, river, or lake may look clean. However, it can still be filled with bacteria, viruses, and parasites that can result in waterborne diseases, such as cryptosporidiosis or giardiasis." (NPS, 2022). They recommend filtering and disinfecting the water before drinking.

Water Filtering image source: Pixabay

Wildfire Mitigation

Having a lake or pond on one's country property would be of great benefit in case of a wildfire. Having a sizable resource of water would be vitally helpful in case of a fire emergency. This could allow helicopters to capture water from the lake to be used for combating the fire. Of course, if your property does not have a resource of standing water, then it would be favorable to have an action plan for the need to defend one's property against an oncoming wildfire or execute an evacuation.

Ideal Country Property

When looking for country property, it would be desirable to find land with some form of surface water. While this is not always possible, it should be high on the wish list when doing the land search.

References

Instructables. (2017, October 8). *How to build a hydraulic Ram Pump.* Autodesk Instructables. https://www.instructables.com/Hoo-to-build-a-Hydraulic-Ram-Pump/

NPS. (2022, August). *Two ways to purify water (U.S. National Park Service).* Two Ways to Purify Water. https://www.nps.gov/articles/2wayspurifywater.htm

Chapter 17: Water Grid – Surface Water

Chapter 18: Water Grid – Water Purification Methods

No matter which type of water source you use on your country property, the water will need to be tested. This is done by purchasing a test kit, either online, or locally. Some counties require the testing to be done by a certified lab.

Testing Water

The typical way water is tested starts with collecting a sample of the water. According to Perfect Pollucon Services, a professional water testing lab, the first step is collecting the sample. They indicate you can have an initial idea of the quality of the water by looking for cloudiness (which is called turbidity), color, odor, and even taste. "Samples are collected in sterile bottles or containers following specific guidelines to prevent contamination." Once at the lab, the sample is checked for chemical parameters, composition, and contamination levels. "pH level measures the acidity or alkalinity of the water and can affect the solubility of substances." The amount of oxygen is also evaluated as well as conductivity. "Conductivity measures the ability of water to conduct electrical current, which can indicate the presence of dissolved solids or salts." They also check for salts, minerals, and other compounds as well as levels of nitrates and phosphates. Evaluations look for heavy metals like lead, mercury, and arsenic. Biological contaminants are watched for such as bacteria, viruses, and fecal coliform or E. coli bacteria. (PPS, 2023).

Test Kits

There is likely a list of local health department approved labs recommending options for testing services. Costs can range from about $15 to hundreds of dollars, so do your research. An example of a nationally-known water testing service is Tap Score. They sell a Core Kit for a home using a private or community-shared well. The kit costs about $200 and tests for over 50 types of contaminants. "This Tap Score test package provides all required materials to properly collect and submit a water sample for certified laboratory testing. The results will include a detailed analysis of common water health concerns related to natural water chemistry and on-premise plumbing. Testing is specialized to address contaminants such as heavy metals, minerals, bacteria, hardness, silica–as well as issues related to plumbing." (Tap Score, 2023).

Addressing Issues

The next critical phase in water treatment is addressing any issues unearthed during testing. It would be very fortunate and extremely rare to have a perfect test result and have no need for filtration or treatment. Each type of treatment is tailored to the specific issues identified in the water test report. That said, there are some people who are blessed with well water that needs no treatment. Following we will look at some of the methods.

Filtration

It is not the purpose of this section to explain portable options for filtering water such as camping water filters or kitchen filters incorporated in pitchers. Rather we are considering a whole-house approach. First off, if you are designing a water system for a new country property, you may choose to split the water into two branches: filtered and unfiltered. The benefit of this approach is that you could save filter replacement costs by only filtering the water that needs to be filtered. For instance, landscape and garden irrigation water does not need filtering in most cases. In the filtration process, the first component the water encounters would likely be a particulate filter unit. This can be configured to include one, two, or three cartridge filters. Below is a sample of a three-cartridge filter design. The actual filters are inside the canister housing. The water first travels through a coarser sediment filter such as 20 microns (shown on the left), then moves to a finer particulate filter such as 5 microns. These two filters are pleated and made of a porous, paper-like material. The third filter is not pleated and not paper-like but is a cylinder with holes in it to let the water circulate through, but this filter is packed with activated carbon with a rating of 1 micron. All three of these filters do not require any electricity to function. You can see that the combination of this series of three filters can capture particulates out of the water in an increasingly finer and finer sequence of filters.

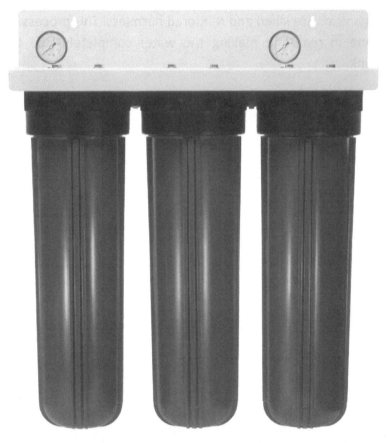

Domestic Water Filters image used with permission from RainHarvest Systems

UV Disinfection

Now that the fine particles in the water have been blocked, the next important treatment is to kill any living organisms. This is done using Ultraviolet (UV) rays. The UV unit shown below is an electrical device made up of a stainless-steel chamber through which the filtered water travels. In the middle of the chamber is a suspended UV tube that is electrically energized. As the water passes the UV light, any organisms are killed and rendered harmless. This process is done in real-time making the water completely safe to drink.

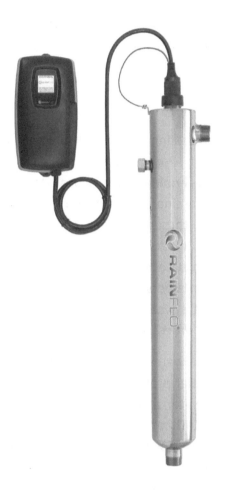

UV Water Treatment image used with permission from
RainHarvest Systems

Once this type of water treatment system is installed, it
would then be favorable to have the treated water tested to
ensure that the final product meets drinking water
standards. Maintenance for this combination of filters and

UV would include replacing filters and the UV bulb as needed or about once a year.

Reverse Osmosis

The initial water testing may identify the need for a different water treatment. Puretec Water explains that "Reverse Osmosis is a technology that is used to remove a large majority of contaminants from water by pushing the water under pressure through a semi-permeable membrane." (Puretec, 2023). Reverse Osmosis (RO) is generally used in homes where bottled water has been preferred over the city water. When a person buys most bottled water or fills up water jugs at a water store, reverse osmoses is usually one of the main processes.

If the source of water is limited, then Reverse Osmosis creates a potential problem. Pureit explains, "For every 1 liter of filtered water, an average RO purifier wastes around 3 liters of water. That indicates that just 25% of the water gets cleansed and 75% of the water is wasted. The amount of water wasted varies depending on the type of RO purifier used." (Pureit, 2023). Usually, reverse osmosis would not be needed on a country property water system.

Removing Iron

Sometimes well water can have iron, resulting in cloudy water and orange stains left on plumbing fixtures. There are three types of iron that can be in well water, and each may have a different treatment approach. The first is ferric iron

170

where the iron particles do not dissolve in the water. Water with the ferric iron present is when you see an orange or rust color in the water or staining the plumbing fixtures. Sediment filters that are smaller than microns can help with this problem.

Ferrous iron, on the other hand, is an iron that is soluble so the water in a glass may appear clear, but as the water is exposed to air and is oxidized, the iron coloration will appear. The treatment method for ferrous iron is a water softener. Sometimes these are used in homes with city water. One example of this treatment approach is using salt. A water softener system will change hard water to soft water. In general, soft water will suds up when washing your hands for instance, while hard water may not. Another way to treat ferrous iron-laden water is a process called manganese greensand. This converts the non-soluble iron into soluble iron which then can be removed in a method known as oxidizing filters.

First Step

There are some other approaches for dealing with iron in water, but that will need further research on the part of the water tester or treatment professional. Likewise, water testing may identify some other issues that we have not discussed here which will need other mitigation efforts. Therefore, the first step in the purification of water for a country home is to have the water tested, to ensure the health and well-being of those drinking the water.

References

PPS. (2023). *Water quality testing procedures.* Perfect
Pollucon Services.
https://www.ppsthane.com/blog/water-quality-
testing-procedures

Tap Score. (2023). *Testing 101.* SimpleLab Tap Score.
https://mytapscore.com/pages/testing-101

Puretec. (2023). *Puretec industrial water: Deionized water
services and reverse osmosis systems.* Reverse
Osmosis | Puretec Industrial Water.
https://puretecwater.com/reverse-osmosis/what-is-
reverse-osmosis

Pureit. (2023). *Best home ro water purifiers online - PUREIT
water india.* pureitwater.com.
https://www.pureitwater.com/blog/post/worried-
about-the-wastage-of-water-while-using-an-ro-
meet-the-ro-water-purifiers-of-the-hour

Chapter 19: Heat Grid – Heating with Wood

When considering a home in the country, there are several options for heating the home. Traditionally, heating options could include natural gas, electric heat, propane, and firewood. We will explore the pros and cons of each of these to show how wood heat would ultimately be the preferred choice for heating a country home, especially during times when one may not be able to buy or sell as we have become accustomed.

Natural Gas Heat

For those in the city or outlying areas such as suburbs, there may be the availability of natural gas. This can be a less expensive method than some other considerations, but it is only available where the gas utility company has plumbed service to the property. Some might be fearful of using natural gas because of a news story they may have seen

174

where the house and surrounding homes in a neighborhood blew up without warning, damaging property and injuring or killing people. For the purpose of this book, natural gas is likely not an option anyway because the goal here is to move away from populated areas, where this resource would likely not be available.

Electric Heaters

Another form of heating is electricity. Older methods of heating with electricity such as wall or baseboard heaters were not very efficient, resulting in higher than necessary electric bills. With the increasing fees per kilowatt hour, using electricity for heat may not be the best choice.

Electric Heat Pumps

Modern electric, whole-house, forced-air furnaces typically utilize a heat pump. The International Energy Agency explains it this way, "A heat pump uses technology similar to that found in a refrigerator or an air conditioner. It extracts heat from a source, such as the surrounding air... then amplifies and transfers the heat to where it is needed. Because most of the heat is transferred rather than generated, heat pumps are far more efficient than conventional heating technologies such as boilers or electric heaters and can be cheaper to run." (IEA, 2023). The advantage of an electric heat pump system is that it's more efficient than wall or baseboard heating systems. It is not the ideal source in a worst-case scenario because you would have no heat if you were unable to acquire electricity due to monetary problems or the grid being down.

Geothermal Electric Heat Pumps

One step more efficient for a heat pump electric furnace is to modify it with a geothermal heat pump. This type of system is also known as a ground source heat pump because of retrieving warmth from underground. The earth is warmer most of the year than the outside air. That temperature differential can be utilized by circulating a refrigerant to pass from the house above ground to long piping deep in the ground. The warmer fluid travels back to the house furnace where the heat exchange takes place. The geothermal heat pump works the same as the conventional heat pump except instead of taking the difference in temperature from the air, it is now taking it from underground. Many times, geothermal piping is buried about eight feet underground. The advantage of a geothermal system is it is more efficient than other electric furnaces and heat pump systems. In a worst-case scenario, it is still not the ideal source for heat since its dependent on electricity.

Mini-Split Electric Heat

A very efficient option for electric heat is called a mini-split or a ductless system. This is area-specific heating, ideal for open-architecture-designed homes and cabins. Gree Comfort explains how a mini-split system is different than a conventional heat pump, "Mini-splits are ductless heating and cooling systems that can be installed in individual rooms or zones throughout a home or business. They consist of an outdoor compressor unit and an indoor air handler that work together to regulate the temperature in each area. This allows homeowners to have precise control over the temperature of each room, without the need for ductwork. The term 'split system' comes from the fact that there is both an outdoor unit and an indoor unit." (Gree, 2023).

Advantages of Mini-Split System

The advantage of choosing a ductless split system is that it is very helpful in lowering the electrical power bill. The disadvantage is that it still requires electricity from the grid. Electricity is not a renewable fuel source, although some might suggest that you could be off-grid and generate your own electricity from solar. Even a very large alternative energy system likely could not provide enough power to meet the demand. The problem is even worse when you need the heat in the winter because winter is when the least electrical power is generated from solar due to shorter daylight hours, overcast days, and less intense sun by being further down on the horizon. The conclusion about heating with any form of electricity is that it is not practical if you are trying to be sustainably independent of the systems of the world. So, we keep considering other options.

Propane Heat

A reasonable heat source to not overlook is a forced-air furnace fueled by propane. This whole house heating method would be much the same as a heat pump equipped electric forced air furnace. They both create heated air in a furnace, passing the heat into different parts of the house through heat ducts. A centrally positioned thermostat controls the house's air temperature. The difference is that propane would be the fuel rather than electricity.

Advantages of Propane Heat

An advantage of propane is that it can be stored long term for later use, unlike electricity. Additionally, propane has an indefinite shelf life, meaning it never goes bad like gasoline does. The disadvantage is that it is not a renewable resource, so may not be available during difficult times once you run out.

Radiant Floor Heating

One unique method of heating a home is radiant floor heating. This approach uses heat from hot water or electricity to heat the floors of a house, which then radiates heat up from the floor to heat the rooms. In an article about radiant heat, Stephanie Cernivec explained, "The biggest benefit of floor-heating systems is their ability to uniformly heat a room and floor. Forced-air heating systems use vents to distribute warm air throughout a room. The location of the vents determines which parts of the room will be warmer than others. In contrast, underfloor radiant heating heats the entire floor, which leads to an evenly heated room and an even ambient temperature around a person's body. This means that you will feel more comfortable at a lower ambient temperature level because you won't experience cold drafts." The article listed additional benefits of radiant floor heating including no maintenance, no noise, being non-allergenic, and energy efficient. (Cernivec, 2022).

Limitations of Radiant Floor Heating

While radiant floor heating is very comfortable, it has some limitations from a sustainable perspective. If the system is heated by a mesh of electrical wires in the floor, then the source of the heat is not a renewable resource. Some might conclude that the electricity could be provided from solar panels as a renewable resource. Any heat generated by electricity is a large draw on a solar electric system. It is very likely impossible to generate enough power to keep up with the needs of this heating system.

When we consider a radiant floor heating system that uses water, one needs to think about what is going to be the heat source for the water. Propane might be an option, but it is not renewable and requires purchasing propane. On the other hand, if the system is heated from a wood furnace, then this could be a viable option.

Wood Heat

Most homesteaders and those off-grid would agree that the heat method of choice is the warmth of a wood stove. Many over the years have appreciated the comfort of the radiant heat from a wood stove. Unlike forced-air furnaces that distribute air through heat ducts, a wood stove provides heat from a single location in the house.

Heat Circulation

In the traditional country home of the past, the woodstove was in the middle of the first floor. Since heat rises, the warm air would circulate to the upper floor without the need of any fan. In a newer home equipped with a forced-air furnace, there would be no heat when the power goes out. A wood stove could be an emergency heat source during a power outage. If a wood stove was the primary method of heating, there is an option to circulate heat throughout a one-story home. In this case, turning on the fan of the forced-air furnace for a few minutes would circulate the air to the ends of the house.

Wood Stove image used with permission from Mary Margaret Eighme

Wood Stoves

Heating with wood is renewable and sustainable. There are several options for heating with wood. First is a fireplace, which is inefficient since most of the warm air easily goes up the chimney. The second option would be to convert the fireplace to a woodstove by adding a woodstove insert. While an air-tight insert is a great improvement to a fireplace it has drawbacks. The amount of heat radiating into the room does not compare to an actual woodstove. An insert only emits heat out the front with the back trapped in the fireplace cavity. A woodstove on the other hand can radiate heat from the front, sides, back, and top. Consequently, the most beneficial type of heating is a free-standing woodstove.

Air-Tight Stoves

Modern woodstoves are air-tight, meaning they are sealed with a gasket around the door. By being air-tight, it allows the owner to completely control the amount of air allowed into the firebox. This results in slower, more efficient burning of the wood, making the length of burn time much longer. An air-tight woodstove, for instance, can burn all night. The traditional stove would require getting up in the night to load more wood. Otherwise, a person would need to start a new fire each morning in a colder house.

Wood Stove image used with permission from Tex and Alline Ladish

Kitchen Wood Stoves

A sustainable alternative to cooking and baking with renewable resources would be a wood-burning kitchen stove. These stoves can resemble the old antique kitchen woodstoves like your grandparents may have had. The newer stoves have many advantages. First, the wood box is usually significantly larger than the old-fashioned ones. In the past, the kitchen woodstove was not for heating the house but simply for supplying the kitchen needs. The firebox was very small, requiring frequent loading of small, kindling-sized pieces of wood. Modern kitchen wood-burning stoves make life much easier with a larger wood box, in some cases even as large as a wood stove. If the kitchen stove is air-tight, it is then possible to heat the entire house as well as burn a fire throughout the night. It would then be possible to heat the house without the need for an additional stove.

Firewood Processing

Firewood is a renewable resource. A homestead would need to have a supply of firewood. You can grow and collect firewood from your property or buy it. The wood can be purchased by truck load for the homeowner to cut and split or purchase firewood ready to stack.

Preferably, your country property would have enough wooded areas that could be a perpetual source of firewood. Ideally, there would be enough timberland to be able to harvest trees that have fallen during the winter storms. This would make it possible to never run out of firewood through the years.

Wood Stove image used with permission from
Steven and Melanie Brundula

Curing Firewood

Unlike sitting around the campfire, wood being burned in a wood stove needs to be cured to burn efficiently and safely. Wood that has not been cured will create creosote when burning, which collects in the chimney and can cause a chimney fire. This is very dangerous. Therefore, firewood needs to be split and stacked in an open area to allow air circulation. This drying time should be long enough to thoroughly cure the wood before stacking it under a roof for year-round storage. A rule of thumb is that firewood should be cured for at least a year to be completely safe and ready for burning in the wood stove. Planning for the needed wood preparation cycle is very important.

Power Tools

Typically, a person would use a chainsaw to cut the logs into blocks into the correct length to fit in the wood stove. Then the blocks would need to be split, so it will dry quicker as well as fit into the woodstove. Splitting is done manually or with a hydraulic log splitter.

Hand Tools

From an emergency or long-term sustainability perspective, the problem with the chainsaw and hydraulic log splitter is that they require purchasing fuel and oil. In a time when petroleum supply is not available, this is a serious problem. Therefore, it would be good to have the needed hand tools to process the firewood. This could include a "misery whip" hand saw for cutting down the tree. Additionally, a small hand saw for bucking the logs into blocks, plus a sledgehammer, a wedge, and an axe to split the blocks are needed. While this method is hard work, it would be a necessary task. This would especially be needed in a time of fuel supply-chain issues or not being able to buy or sell.

Renewable Heat

We have seen that while there are several ways to heat a home, burning wood is about the only way to heat using renewable energy and more importantly heating using a source that is on your own property. This allows you to have the comfort of wood heat as well as a perpetual supply of that renewable resource.

References

IEA. (2023). *How a heat pump works – the future of heat pumps – analysis*. International Energy Agency. https://www.iea.org/reports/the-future-of-heat-pumps/how-a-heat-pump-works

Gree. (2023). *Mini-splits vs heat pumps: Understanding the differences*. GREE Comfort. https://www.greecomfort.com/news-and-events/mini-splits-vs-heat-pumps/

Cernivec, S. (2022, June 29). *9 pros & cons of heated floors that will surprise you*. WarmlyYours.com. https://www.warmlyyours.com/en-US/posts/9-pros-and-cons-of-heated-floors

Additional Video and Podcast Resources

www.preparingforthetimeoftrouble.com - Part 73
"Firewood When You Can't Buy or Sell"

www.preparingforthetimeoftrouble.com – Part 340
"Sharpening a Chainsaw"

www.preparingforthetimeoftrouble.com – Part 341
"Firewood Cutting Hand Tools"

www.preparingforthetimeoftrouble.com – Part 342
"Splitting Firewood"

Chapter 19: Heat Grid – Heating with Wood

Chapter 20: Information Grid- Face-to-Face

Technology is moving forward exponentially. We are so accustomed to having the world in our pockets. Our smartphone literally is not only a phone, but a computer, and an Internet-connected device. We can hardly remember when it was not that way. While some readers of this book may be young enough to never have seen a time when there no cell phones, some of us more seasoned individuals do remember.

Proliferation of Smartphones

While even in third-world countries, the proliferation of smartphones is surprising. In countries where you might expect everything to be backward and out of date, cell phones are becoming more and more common. With smartphones, now you can literally do almost everything you could do online from a computer but have the mobility and convenience of having it in your hand.

Face-to-Face Communication image source: Pixabay

Advances in Connectivity

The advances in Internet connectivity are mind-boggling. Internet services can now be global in reach. The earth is being surrounded by satellite links so that it is possible to have an Internet connection from remote locations that previously were out of reach. When considering cell phones and Internet access, the amount of data that is right at our fingertips is truly amazing.

GPS

GPS technology has now become commonplace allowing us to use our smartphones to help us navigate traffic, find the best price for the next stop for fuel, and get hands-free directions to our destination. It was not long ago that buying a new car with a navigation screen embedded in our dash was stylish, futuristic, and helpful. Now with the smartphone, an in-dash navigation system seems to be unnecessary.

Digitizing for Profit

Some of us remember pay phones on almost every corner. Now if you find a phone booth, it is most likely missing the phone. With cell phone numbers being unlisted by default and Google being able to find anything you want, the printed Yellow Pages are a thing of the past. Other printed media such as newspapers and magazines have had the same challenge. Many major printing mega operations that have failed to figure out how to digitize for profit, have all but vanished.

What If?

All of these wonderful technological conveniences are dependent on one thing - electricity. What if the grid went down for good? What if there was no longer any cell service? What if the Internet was unavailable? How handicapped would you be?

Connection Dependent

Most of us spend an inordinate amount of time on our devices, whether a laptop or a mobile device. I would imagine that each of us would be amazed if we actually could accurately log each minute we are using our technological devices! For me at least, I think I would be lost and have withdrawals if I could not be connected.

Disconnected Society

At the same time, as a result, our society has changed due to the amount of time using our devices. We have, in many ways, become disconnected from each other. I often chuckle recalling seeing a TV show of two teenage girls walking down the hall at school, ignoring each other because they were texting. Only to find out that they were texting each other, even though they were walking shoulder to shoulder next to each other. What a sad commentary of our modern lives.

Learning to Communicate Face-to-Face

Again, what if there was no electricity, no Internet, and no cell service? What then? We would need to learn to communicate with each other all over again. Imagine families eating dinner together and talking about their day without the interruption of a notification of a call, text, or news flash in real time!

The Impact of Life-Alerting Changes

Facts are our lives, as we know them, could change with little or no warning. Most of us have never lived in a war-torn country, let alone a nuclear war. What about an electromagnetic pulse (EMP)? An EMP is considered the first strike of some enemy or rogue nations before an all-out war. An EMP could shut down the grid and potentially disable most electronics. This scenario is predicted to set America back a hundred or more years.

Monetary System Interruption

What if the monetary system was disabled due to a terrorist hack? What if you could not buy or sell? Even if the connectivity of cell and Internet were possible, you would not be able to pay for these services. Any of these what-ifs are frightening.

Fortunately, at least we could talk to our family members and neighbors without any technological crutches. That kind of quiet world might provide a much less stressful and peaceful life. Time will tell.

Additional Video and Podcast Resources

www.preparingforthetimeoftrouble.com - Part 63
"Living Without Electricity"

Chapter 21: Financial Grid- Cashless Society

Many people are concerned about the stability of America's financial system. We can be reminded from the past how things can change seemingly overnight. The stock market crash in 1929 resulted in ten years of soup lines and massive unemployment during the Great Depression. The housing and banking collapse of 2008, named by some as the Great Recession, resulted in thousands of individuals losing large percentages of their financial worth, and untold numbers of houses were repossessed due to default.

Financial Collapses

Forbes magazine explained how gold finally was not equated to the value of the U.S. dollar, "In August 1971, President Richard Nixon formally unpegged the U.S. dollar from gold, meaning the greenback was no longer convertible into bullion. Overnight, the dollar became a free-floating currency, measurable only by comparing it to other world currencies. And yet there were still restrictions on private ownership of gold coins, bars and the like. It wouldn't be until President Gerald Ford signed a bill in December 1974 that Americans could freely buy and trade bullion, for the first time in over 40 years." (Holmes, 2022).

New York Stock Exchange image source: Library of Congress

Fiat Currency

Currently, the US dollar is fiat currency. Investopedia explains, "Fiat money is a government-issued currency that is not backed by a commodity such as gold. Fiat money gives central banks greater control over the economy because they can control how much money is printed. Most modern paper currencies, such as the U.S. dollar, are fiat currencies." (Chen, 2023). As a result, we have seen that when there is a need for more currency, more money is just printed. This practice is not sustainable and will have long-term implications.

US Dollar and the Global Standard

We now hear rumblings of the US dollar being threatened by no longer being the world standard. According to Global Times, "Chinese yuan may replace the US dollar as the world's reserve and settlement ...China is now the world's second-largest economy and will soon become the first." (Times, 2023).

Banking Sector Vulnerabilities

Banks in the tech sector of Silicon Valley have defaulted and the banking system seems to show signs of free fall. According to a report by the Social Science Research Network, "186 banks in the United States are at risk of failure or collapse due to rising interest rates and a high proportion of uninsured deposits." (Santarelli, 2023).

Plastic Money

More and more we are dependent on plastic forms of payment with credit or debit cards. Increasingly we are seeing large store chains expanding their self-checkout aisles, saving employee labor costs, and increasing the use of cashless means of transactions.

What To Do?

With the seeming lack of stability in our monetary system, one might wonder what the result of a total financial meltdown and collapse would be. What would you do if you were unable to access your savings and checking account funds in your bank? For these and other reasons, people are taking their cash out of banks and stuffing it under the proverbial mattress or in a safe. Some are investing in gold and silver, which in turn is stored somewhere considered safe.

If our country finds itself in the throes of a global, nuclear war, we could discover our assets frozen in the name of stabilizing the country. In the case of an EMP shutting down the grid, all traditional transactions would come to an immediate halt. Delivery trucks would not move, due to the inability to pump fuel. Goods in stores would no longer be available for purchase because the electronic transaction machines would not operate without power and Internet connectivity. What would you do then?

Worthless Paper Money

What if the federal government changed from fiat paper money to some form of digital currency? There likely would be a deadline to turn in your cash, after which the coins and paper money could be worthless. The only exception might be very old and rare coins that were made of gold or silver. Of course, these likely have been snatched up over the years by collectors and preppers.

Gold Coins image source: Pixabay

Gold and Silver

Even having gold and silver can have its drawbacks because how would you be able to exchange a gold or silver coin for some purchase that was valued at less or more of the face value of the precious metal? Things could get complicated.

The Barter System

The final, last resort could be the barter system. The Economic Times explains the origins of this way of making transactions, "Before the hard currency came into existence, the most common form of trade was bartering. The Barter System dates back to the old time when there was no money. The only way to buy goods was to exchange them with personal belongings of similar value." (TET, 2023). Bartering could be in the form of trading many things, as compared to making purchases with cash. Bartering is exchanging anything of value for something one needs. For instance, you might have some extra firewood and your neighbor might have some form of food you need. Bartering can include exchanging goods for services, such as a needed tool for doing some physical labor. Of course, if a person has stashed away precious metals, these can be exchanged for goods or services needed. While there are many ways to barter, the main missing ingredient is cash.

As we contemplate the various vulnerabilities of our present economic system, it is time well-spent to consider alternatives to our financial grid, if there might be a temporary or long-term, catastrophic financial collapse to our modern way of financial transactions.

References

Holmes, F. (2022a, November 9). *The gold standard ended 50 years ago. federal debt has only exploded since.* Forbes. https://www.forbes.com/sites/greatspeculations/2021/01/25/the-gold-standard-ended-50-years-ago-federal-debt-has-only-exploded-since/?sh=46f5afa71e17

Chen, J. (2023). *Fiat Money: What it is, how it works, example, Pros & Cons.* Investopedia. https://www.investopedia.com/terms/f/fiatmoney.asp

Times. (2023). *VTB chairman: Yuan to replace Dollar as Main Reserve currency in future.* Global Times. https://www.globaltimes.cn/page/202305/1291336.shtml

Santarelli, M. (2023a, September 2). *Which Banks Are in Danger of Failing or Collapse?.* Norada Real Estate Investments. https://www.noradarealestate.com/blog/which-banks-are-in-danger-of-failing/

TET (2023). *What is barter? definition of barter, barter meaning.* The Economic Times. (2023). https://economictimes.indiatimes.com/definition/barter

Additional Video and Podcast Resources

www.preparingforthetimeoftrouble.com - Part 43
"Country Living on a Budget – Money Saving Tips"

Chapter 22: Medical Grid- Homestead Remedies

While we continue our consideration of the different kinds of "grids" that we depend on in our modern society, the medical grid is a very important one. We all depend on doctors and other medical professionals to help keep us healthy. We also rely on hospitals and emergency rooms for those unforeseen interruptions in our normal daily routine. Whether we are fortunate enough to have medical insurance or if we are depending on other methods for access to medical services, we all somehow find a way to get taken care of in those times of medical distress.

Medical Services

Healthcare professionals we depend on are trained, educated, and skilled. Some health services provided include laboratory, diagnostic, and preventative care. We trust our doctor's judgment and recommendations for our well-being.

Worst-Case Scenarios

What if a time came when we were unable to have skilled level of medical care? We have been contemplating worst-case scenarios and their impacts on other "grids". Medical services may not be available during a nuclear attack, an EMP, or total power grid failure. Where would you then turn for medical help? Do you expect the government to take care of you in these catastrophic events?

Do you have anyone in your family or circle of friends who has medical knowledge during these times of dire need? If not, how much do you know about other forms of medical diagnoses and alternative health treatments?

Learn While You Can

It might be desirable for you to attempt to learn about ways to analyze your own medical situations. Evaluate what you have at your fingertips and what you might need to treat a variety of medical situations. Consider what supplies you might already have in your home that could be helpful. These may include bandages, ointments, salves, activated charcoal, hydrogen peroxide, and aloe vera, just to name a few. Where should you start to get suggestions of supplements and alternative treatments to have in your medical war chest?

Herbal Remedies image: Pixabay

Items to Have on Hand

Healthline suggests nine home remedies that are backed by science to have on hand. "Turmeric for pain and inflammation. ... Chili peppers for pain and soreness ... Ginger for pain and nausea ... Shiitake mushrooms for the long game ... Eucalyptus oil for pain relief ... Lavender for migraine and anxiety ... Mint for muscle pain and digestion ... Fenugreek for breastfeeding." (Escandon, 2023). Some of these items you may already have in your kitchen cabinet. It would be good to make a list of these items and where they are in your house. Consider buying what you do not already have and add them to your available resources.

Wild Medicinal Plants

There may be a time when you need one or more of these home remedies. During difficult times you may find that you are missing some of the items. It would be good to have learned alternative ways to utilize these important natural remedies. You may find it helpful to know other medicinal plants you could identify in the wild and forage in the woods. An example would be mint, which grows wild near wet areas such as along a riverbank.

Kitchen Spice Rack

Many of these items are seasonings for cooking and could be added to your kitchen spice rack, if for no other reason than for medicinal treatment in an emergency. Ginger can help with morning sickness. I personally took ginger snap cookies on an open ocean boat trip to help with motion sickness. Being nauseated is not fun! Ginger reportedly is good for headaches and pain relief as well.

Other Remedies

Shiitake mushrooms are reportedly helpful in boosting a person's immune system by consuming some each day. Eucalyptus oil can be purchased as an essential oil and may be helpful with congestion and relief of body pain. Lavender is good for dealing with anxiety and headaches, and if in essential oil form, can be used as aroma therapy by misting it into the air and breathing it. Fenugreek is a spice that reportedly can help with diarrhea and managing blood sugar.

One Size Does Not Fit All

As with all treatments, there is no "one size fits all". When trying some new topical or oral treatments, always do your own research and start with small amounts. Watch for negative reactions and only increase when deemed safe to do so.

Cautions

WebMD has this appropriate caution, "No matter what you've heard or how badly you want relief, talk with your doctor or pharmacist before trying any home remedy. This is even more important if you take prescription or over-the-counter medications, because some can affect how drugs work." (WebMD, 2023).

Plan Ahead

Of course, during normal times it is advisable to consult with your primary care physician before introducing anything new medically. In a worst-case scenario such medical help may no longer be available. Your wellbeing may depend on that knowledge and experience.

Disclaimer

This chapter is not meant to be medical advice. Be sure to do your own due diligence and consult with your doctor before trying any natural remedy treatments.

References

Escandon, R. (2023, June 1). *9 Home Remedies Backed by Science*. Healthline.
https://www.healthline.com/health/home-remedies

WebMD. (2023). *Home Remedies That Work*. WebMD.
https://www.webmd.com/balance/ss/slideshow-home-remedies

Additional Video and Podcast Resources

www.preparingforthetimeoftrouble.com – Homestead Remedies Section - Presentations about using wild plants, herbs, hydrotherapy, fresh air, sunlight, and exercise to boost your immune system and overall health.

Chapter 22: Medical Grid - Homestead Remedies

Chapter 23: Medical Grid-Emergency Preparedness

Some time ago several families were together and discussing emergency preparedness. One suggested that we do an exercise to analyze how well-prepared we each were. This was not preplanned or rehearsed by anyone, including the person who made the suggestion.

Emergency Scenario

The idea was that we all go out to our vehicles and show what, if any, emergency preparedness items we might have in our cars. The suggested scenario was that an EMP had just hit and without any sound or warning had taken down the power grid. We were each supposedly 30 miles from our homes. There was no way of knowing how long this power outage would last. Therefore, we agreed that the best course of action was to attempt to return to our respective homes. As the vehicles were all newer models, with some form of computerization, none of the cars would run, so our only option was to walk 30 miles on foot.

Available Vehicle Emergency Items

The big question was, what did we each previously include in our vehicles that might be useful in this kind of emergency? We all watched as each vehicle was opened, and the useful items were revealed. To my surprise, everyone had something helpful. In this mock scenario, the problem was each of us were independent and could not share supplies.

Power Outage image: Pixabay

Truth Revealed

One person was very well prepared, with a bin full of emergency supplies for their family of four. The rest of us were in trouble due to having inadequate provisions on hand. This was a moment of truth and proved to be a very revealing exercise from which we all learned a valuable lesson. Think ahead and be prepared!

Getting Back Home

This mock scenario focused on the idea of being able to safely travel 30 miles to reach our respective homes. In an unexpected grid-down situation, getting home would be very important. For one thing, this would be the best place for riding out a situation with no power. Secondly, a person would want to protect their home from damage due to not having power, such as freezing pipes or other unexpected issues. It would also be important to reunite with other family members to plan and work together to move forward with an action plan. Lastly, being at your property would allow you to defend it from potential looters.

Types of Emergency Preparation

While this unplanned exercise was about traveling home on foot and likely having to spend the night out in the open, there are other kinds of situations that warrant planning in advance. The focus of this chapter is on emergency medical preparation. While the traveling back home situation would need to include some limited medical-related needs, we will now look at being better prepared for a multi-faceted array of medical emergencies.

Medical Emergency

The American Red Cross suggests three steps in being ready for an emergency: have an emergency kit, make a plan, and be informed. They recommend, "Learn the essential supplies to put in your family's survival kit...Plan effectively for you and your family in case of emergency...Understand which disasters are likely to occur in your area and what you must know to stay safe." (Red Cross, 2023).

You Think You're Ready?

The Red Cross further suggests a way to test yourself and what your response would be to the following critical statements:

"1 - I know what emergencies or disasters are most likely to occur in my community.

2 - I have a family disaster plan and have practiced it.

3 - I have a survival kit.

4 - At least one member of my household is trained in first aid and CPR/AED. I have taken action to help my community prepare." (Red Cross, 2023).

Expanded First Aid Kit

The Mayo Clinic recommends buying a first aid kit but adding items that might be missing from the following suggested items:

"Basic supplies

- Adhesive tape
- Elastic wrap bandages
- Bandage strips and "butterfly" bandages in assorted sizes
- Super glue
- Rubber tourniquet or 16 French catheter
- Nonstick sterile bandages and roller gauze in assorted sizes
- Eye shield or pad
- Large triangular bandage (may be used as a sling)
- Aluminum finger splint
- Instant cold packs
- Cotton balls and cotton-tipped swabs
- Disposable non-latex examination gloves, several pairs
- Duct tape
- Petroleum jelly or other lubricant
- Plastic bags, assorted sizes
- Safety pins in assorted sizes
- Scissors and tweezers
- Hand sanitizer
- Antibiotic ointment
- Antiseptic solution and towelettes
- Eyewash solution
- Thermometer

- Turkey baster or other bulb suction device for flushing wounds
- Sterile saline for irrigation, flushing
- Breathing barrier (surgical mask)
- Syringe, medicine cup, or spoon
- First-aid manual
- Hydrogen peroxide to disinfect

Medications

- Aloe vera gel
- Calamine lotion
- Anti-diarrhea medication
- Laxative
- Antacids
- Antihistamine, such as diphenhydramine
- Hydrocortisone cream
- Cough and cold medications
- Personal medications that don't need refrigeration
- Auto-injector of epinephrine, if prescribed by your doctor
- Pain relievers, such as acetaminophen (Tylenol, others), ibuprofen (Advil, Motrin IB, others)" (Mayo, 2022).

First Aid and CPR Training

It would be a good idea to update your first aid certificate by taking a Red Cross first aid and CPR refresher course. Remembering how to administer assistance and open breathing passageways can be life-saving skills. If it has been a while since that type of training, a person might forget how to do CPR during a moment of crisis, so planning ahead and being proactive can be vitally important.

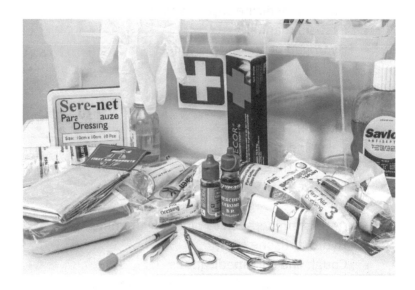

First Aid Kit image source: Pixabay

Having a Plan of Action

To be prepared for any type of emergency, it would be helpful to have a plan of action in a moment of crisis. For instance, if there is a wildfire heading toward your home and your family members are not together at that moment, it would be a good idea to have already agreed on a location to meet. Personally, our family has two agreed locations: one is on the home property and the other is off-site some distance away. By having both identified rendezvous points preestablished one can be sure to be able to reconnect with loved ones during times of disaster.

Being Prepared

You can see from this mock scenario that it is a good idea to do some preplanning to be prepared for an unforeseen crisis. Emergency items in your vehicle could be vitally important. An extensive First Aid kit would be needed when a medical emergency arises. Having an action plan will ensure that your family members know what to do in the event of an unexpected crisis.

References

Red Cross. (2023). *How To Prepare For Emergencies*. How to Prepare for Emergencies | Be Red Cross Ready | Red Cross. https://www.redcross.org/get-help/how-to-prepare-for-emergencies.html

Mayo. (2022, July 13). *First-aid kits: Stock supplies that can save lives*. Mayo Clinic. https://www.mayoclinic.org/first-aid/first-aid-kits/basics/art-20056673

Additional Video and Podcast Resources

www.preparingforthetimeoftrouble.com - Part 61 "Bug Out Bags"

www.preparingforthetimeoftrouble.com - Part 255 "Making a Car Emergency Kit"

www.preparingforthetimeoftrouble.com - Part 266 "Surviving a Winter Power Outage"

www.preparingforthetimeoftrouble.com – Part 326 "Backcountry Medical Aid"

Chapter 24: EMP Dangers and Precautions

An Electromagnetic Pulse, known as an EMP, has been the backbone of several doomsday movies. While the films may over-dramatize the event and the aftermath, the threat of an EMP attack on the United States is very real. An EMP is caused by a high-altitude detonation of a nuclear bomb. If centrally positioned over the continental US, it has the potential to destroy all microelectronics as well as take down the nation's electrical power grid.

EMP image source: Pixabay

North Korea and EMPs

A report by the EMP Task Force on National and Homeland Security stated that "North Korea's KMS-3 and KMS-4 satellites orbit over the U.S. daily. Their trajectory is similar to that planned for a Soviet-era secret weapon called the Fractional Orbital Bombardment System (FOBS) deployed by the USSR to make a surprise High-altitude EMP (HEMP) attack on the United States. Trajectories of North Korea's KMS-3 and KMS-4 satellites are near optimal for a HEMP attack on the U.S., if they are nuclear-armed." (Fry, 2021).

China and EMPs

Regarding the risks of China being able to detonate an EMP, the EMP Task Force stated that "China has long known about nuclear high-altitude electromagnetic pulse (HEMP) and invested in protecting military forces and critical infrastructures from HEMP and other nuclear weapon effects during the Cold War and continuing today. China has HEMP simulators and defensive and offensive programs that are almost certainly more robust than any in the United States. China's military doctrine regards nuclear HEMP attack as an extension of information or cyber warfare, and deserving highest priority as the most likely kind of future warfare." (EMP Task Force, 2020).

Russia and EMPs

With the attack on Ukraine by Russia continuing, in a 2022 Forbes article, James Broughel stated, "Vladimir Putin may be considering a nuclear attack Ukraine—but not the kind you think...Russia might instead detonate a bomb far up in the atmosphere, unleashing an electromagnetic pulse (EMP) that destroys nearly all electronics on the ground within a radius of hundreds, or even thousands of miles." (Broughel, 2022). If Russia did detonate an EMP over Ukraine, this would be the first military use of an EMP as a weapon against an enemy.

Regarding Russia's possible use of an EMP against the United States, in a paper by Jean Bele, from the Laboratory for Nuclear Science at MIT, the following was stated, "China and Russia have also considered limited nuclear attack options that, unlike their Cold War plan, employ EMP as the primary or sole means of attack. Indeed, as recently as May 1999, during the NATO bombing of the former Yugoslavia, high-ranking members of the Russian Duma, meeting with a U.S. congressional delegation to discuss the Balkans conflict, raised the specter of a Russian EMP attack that would paralyze the United States." (Bele, 2004).

The U.S. Naval Institute explained, "Russia and China have the ability to destroy the U.S. power grid and degrade military capabilities with a nonkinetic first strike—not only through the electromagnetic effects of nuclear and nonnuclear weapons, but also by means such as cyberattacks." (Owen, 2023).

Terrorists and EMPs

Even as far back as the year 2000, a special United States oversight panel on terrorism claimed that, "Nuclear terrorism, regarded as the stuff of fictional novels and movies during the Cold War, is now widely regarded as plausible...Terrorists armed with short-range missiles, which these days can be purchased even by arms collectors and museums on the international market and armed with nuclear weapons, could conceivably make an electronic attack against the United States. An electromagnetic pulse (EMP) attack could incapacitate power grids, communications, computer systems, and even electronic infrastructure that makes modern society possible." (SOPOT, 2000).

Power Grid Down image source: Pixabay

What to Do?

With the possibility of an EMP being detonated over the United States by North Korea, China, Russia, or even a rogue terrorist, the results could be catastrophic, disabling the electrical power grid, all forms of communication, computers, and anything with microelectronics. This would include almost anything electronic from cars to planes, to cell phones to medical equipment. Is there anything that can be done to circumvent the destruction of your own needed devices?

The Faraday Cage

It is difficult to perfectly anticipate the impact of an EMP because there has never been a modern EMP detonated during our age of high dependence on electronics. Many have educated guesses of what can be done. The main preventative measure that is known is the shielding of electronics. This can be done with what is called a Faraday cage. This metal box is designed to protect electronics from the harmful rays emitted by an EMP.

Building a Faraday Cage

While purchasing a commercially-made Faraday cage can be very expensive, one electrical engineer suggested a simple and inexpensive method by using nested metal garbage cans. For a video of the step-by-step process of building a homemade Faraday cage, see the links at the end of the chapter. Even if this method of protecting your electronic devices is not a completely fool-proof method of fortification, any attempt is better than doing nothing at all.

What to Put in a Faraday Cage?

Askaprepper.com website suggested some potential items to consider protecting by storing in a Faraday cage: 2-way communication radio, CB radio, portable AM/FM radio, shortwave radio, ham radio, solar battery charger, and a LED flashlight. (Jorgustin, 2022). If you have a solar alternative energy system, you may wish to purchase spare electronic components in case the EMP disables your solar system charge controller and inverter. This may mean you will need more than one Faraday cage to have the space to store these added components. It is believed that solar panels and batteries will likely withstand the impact of an EMP so they would probably not need Faraday protection.

Protecting Your Power Panel

There has never been an EMP in modern times so it is hard to tell what protection will work. One additional device available for purchase is an apparatus that protects your house's breaker panel. This component is installed in the breaker panel and intercepts the power coming into the panel from the grid. The goal is for that piece of equipment to be sacrificed rather than the destruction of everything in the house.

Real Threat

Once again, no one knows for sure the effectiveness of attempts to protect against an EMP since there has never been a modern-time detonation of an EMP. One thing we do know, there is a real threat of an EMP as a first strike in an attack on the United States. Anything we can do to protect ourselves is worth a try.

References

Fry, P. V. (2021, June 6). *NORTH KOREA: EMP THREAT - DTIC.* North Korea's Capabilities for Electromagnetic (EMP) Attack. https://apps.dtic.mil/sti/trecms/pdf/AD1135779.pdf

EMP Task Force. (2023, February 6). *China EMP Threat: The People's Republic of China Military Doctrine, Plans, and Capabilities for Electromagnetic Pulse (EMP) Attack: Public Intelligence.* China EMP Threat. https://publicintelligence.net/us-china-emp-threat/

Broughel, J. (2022, November 18). *Would Putin Launch An Electromagnetic Pulse Attack Against Ukraine?.* Forbes. https://www.forbes.com/sites/jamesbroughel/2022/11/18/would-putin-launch-an-electromagnetic-pulse-attack-against-ukraine/?sh=3f308cab48dd

Bele, J. M. (2004). *Nuclear Weapons Education Project.* High altitude electromagnetic pulse (EMP) attack scenario against the USA | Nuclear Weapons Education Project. https://nuclearweaponsedproj.mit.edu/high-altitude-electromagnetic-pulse-emp-attack-scenario-against-usa

Owen, J. (2023, February 14). *An EMP or Solar Incident Could Result in Blackout Warfare .* U.S. Naval Institute. https://www.usni.org/magazines/proceedings/2023/february/emp-or-solar-incident-could-result-blackout-warfare

SOPOT - Special Oversight Panel on Terrorism. (2000, May 23). *Terrorist Threats to the United States*. Terrorist Threats to the United States. https://commdocs.house.gov/committees/security/has144240.000/has144240_0f.htm

Jorgustin, K. (2022, March 30). *What To Store In A Faraday Cage For EMP Protection?*. Ask a Prepper. https://www.askaprepper.com/what-to-store-in-a-faraday-cage-for-emp-protection/

Additional Video and Podcast Resources

www.preparingforthetimeoftrouble.com - Part 6 "EMP Dangers and Prevention"

www.preparingforthetimeoftrouble.com - Part 317 "EMP Preparedness"

Chapter 24: EMP Dangers and Precautions

Chapter 25: Food Grid – Year-Round Food Supply

After many years of developing and expanding our gardens, we asked ourselves the question of whether we thought we had enough food production to live off for a year. Even though there were only two mouths to feed, our conclusion was not even close! Food for a year, of course, requires various methods to store and preserve food for the off-season. In subsequent chapters, we will address several well-known gardening methods, how to save seeds from year to year, food preservation methods, extending the growing season, as well as how big of a garden is needed for a self-sustainable country home.

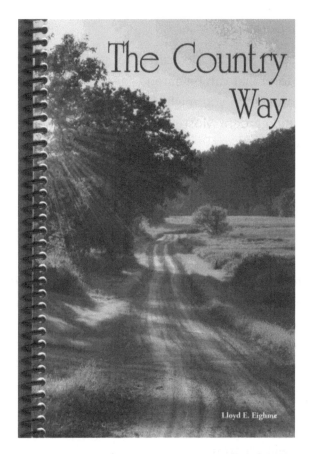

The Country Way Book Cover image used with permission
from Mary Margaret Eighme

Seasonal Gardening

This chapter will be dedicated to growing a garden to provide food that can be eaten year-round. If you live near the equator, then you might be able to grow a productive year-round garden. Most of the world has four seasons to contend with.

Right Plant. Right Conditions

In the northern hemisphere, spring and summer are the main growing seasons. Select cool season and warm season crops for your gardening zone. Harvesting is during the summer and fall, depending on the variety, germination cycle, and time of reaching maturity. Some plants grow better in warmer weather such as watermelon, while others prefer a cooler environment. Irrigation is essential in the garden. A person would need to select the watering techniques and frequency based on the needs of each plant type and region. You will learn by trial and error about your local growing season.

Seasonal Eating

Eat fresh produce from your garden that is in season for your geographic area. Learn how to preserve fruits and vegetables for use during the off-season. Rather than planting too many varieties, be sure to plant what you like to eat.

Supply Chain Shortages

As explained in an earlier chapter, it was a wake-up call to our family when my wife one morning went to her favorite grocery store to find the produce shelves bare. What a shock! The reality is that garden produce does not have a long shelf life so is generally delivered daily. An interruption in the supply chain would have immediate ramifications. It is important to be able to grow your own food. Not only do you have control of the supply, but the flavor and nutritional value is noticeably better with food from your garden. Growing your own food is a valuable resource.

Staggered Harvesting

A person should learn to stagger the planting dates to extend the harvest times. If produce needs to be picked at the same time, it would be difficult to take advantage of the harvest with the time-consuming preservation methods. A homestead.org article by Jenny Flores, suggests that succession planting is an important way to have a more productive garden and stagger the harvesting, "Succession planting is a highly effective technique used to maximize harvests. Essentially, you will quickly fill the space left by a harvested crop with a new crop. Stagger plantings at 1-2 week intervals and replace early crops with summer crops, followed quickly by fall and winter crops. If you create a succession planting calendar and stick to it, you can harvest and replant quick-growing crops up to four times a season." (Flores, 2023). She suggests supplementing food supply during the winter with growing microgreens.

Year-Round Gardening

An article written by Benedict Vanheems suggests six proven ways to grow year-round by first implementing gardening techniques to extend the growing season. The next suggestion is to overwinter vegetables. He explains, "You may be surprised at what will grow throughout the winter: salads such as mizuna, tatsoi, endive, winter lettuce, and mustards; leafy greens including chard, spinach, and the every-ready kale; plus all manner of overwintered carrots, parsnip, beets, and leeks. Even colder climates can produce a cornucopia of pickings given the protection of a cold frame or greenhouse." (Vanheems, 2017). For the time when harvests are scant, springtime can fill the 'hungry gap' with vegetables you would have planted the previous summer: leeks, cabbage, and broccoli. Lastly, make an early start in the spring with hearty plants like chard, onions and cabbage. Some techniques can give your plants a head start, like doing starts indoors under grow lights. Another approach is to prewarm the soil in a greenhouse to get a jump start on successful planting. (Vanheems, 2017).

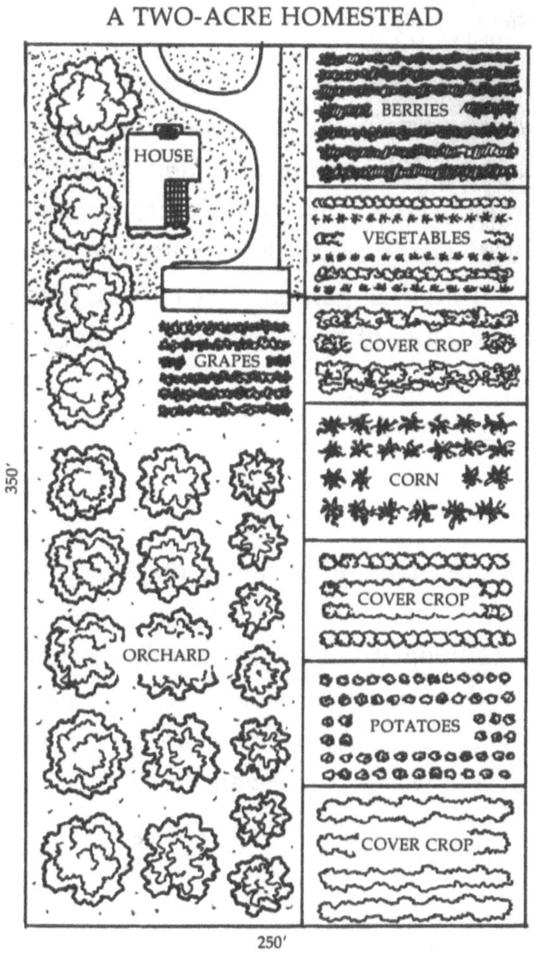

A TWO-ACRE HOMESTEAD

BERRIES

HOUSE

VEGETABLES

GRAPES

COVER CROP

350'

CORN

COVER CROP

ORCHARD

POTATOES

COVER CROP

250'

Year-Round Food Supply Plan image used with permission
from Mary Margaret Eighme

Lessons From the Past

You may recall early in this book the story was told of Lloyd Eighme who was a child during the Great Depression. By careful planning, his parents were able to provide for the needs of their family from strategic use of their two-acre property. With eggs from chickens, milk from their one cow, and harvest from their garden, they made it through those tough times by lots of hard work and using every part of their land.

Preserving Methods

Methods of preserving food can be done by freeze-drying, dehydrating, fermentation, freezing, pressure canning and water bath canning. While freezing produce requires having a freezer, other methods include storing produce in a pantry or a cellar. Glass canning jars would need to be stored in such a way as to prevent freezing on the coldest days of winter.

Planning for the Worst

If you live in an area that might ever have an earthquake, it would be good to consider the security of stored food items on shelves. This might mean adding some strips of wood or string to the shelving to prevent the jars from falling during the seismic event.

In the following chapters, we will introduce several gardening methods, how to save seeds, ways to preserve food, how to extend your growing season, plus consider the size of a garden needed for self-sustainable country living.

References

Flores, J. (2023, February 9). *12 Months of Fresh Produce: How to Grow Food All Year*. Homestead.org. https://www.homestead.org/gardening/how-to-grow-food-all-year/

Vanheems, B. (2017, October 27). *6 Proven Strategies for Year-round Harvests*. GrowVeg. https://www.growveg.com/guides/6-proven-strategies-for-year-round-harvests/

Additional Video and Podcast Resources

www.preparingforthetimeoftrouble.com - Part 18
"How Big a Garden When You Can't Buy or Sell?"

www.preparingforthetimeoftrouble.com - Part 27
"Preserving Food by Canning When You Can't Buy or Sell"

www.preparingforthetimeoftrouble.com - Part 37
"Emergency and Long-Term Food Storage"

www.preparingforthetimeoftrouble.com - Part 42
"Drying Food When You Can't Buy or Sell"

www.preparingforthetimeoftrouble.com - Part 74
"Pantries and Cold Rooms"

www.preparingforthetimeoftrouble.com - Part 189
"Storing Food Without Electricity"

Chapter 25: Food Grid – Year-Round Food Supply

Chapter 26: Food Grid – Gardening: Back to Eden Method

Growing up in Los Angeles Paul Gautschi learned to love gardening, even though it was hard work having to till the clay soil and adding horse manure. As an adult, Paul moved his young family to the Olympic Peninsula of Washington State. He once again attempted to continue his love of gardening but experienced new struggles by not having enough water from their 200-plus deep well. How could he possibly garden successfully on this property with the hardship of not having enough water?

Look Up

One day he was contemplating this problem and talking to God, he says that God told him he was looking in the wrong place. He looked up and noticed the trees in the woods were healthy and sustaining themselves without any outside assistance. He then looked at the ground around the base of the trees and noticed that the top layer was light, fluffy, moist compost. Paul there discovered what later he would call the "Back to Eden" method of gardening.

Self-Sustaining

Paul says, "When God designed the landscape project for planet Earth, He was so genius He designed it in such as way that He would never have to show up to work. It is completely self-sustained." (Back to Eden, 2020). With the Back to Eden concept in mind he applied what he saw in the woods to the new orchard he was planting. At first he used straw and sheep manure, then later adding decomposing trimmings from trees.

Garden image used with permission from Back to Eden

No Water or Fertilizer

At the time of filming the *Back to Eden* documentary movie, he had the orchard for over 30 years and never once had to water or fertilize it. Despite the amazing success with the orchard, he did not use this method in his vegetable garden. He was a creature of habit, growing the vegetable garden the traditional way with hard work, continual labor and adding amendments. He was frustrated because in the spring the ground was muddy and wet. After tilling, the garden would be full of weeds in a matter of days.

No Weeds

One day he looked at the ground in the orchard and realized it had no weeds and was moist compost-- all without any labor! He realized that this concept could work in the vegetable garden as well. He threw away his tiller and from then on, the only tool he used was a rake.

Garden of Eden

In the Garden of Eden, the garden was lush and beautiful, without thorns or hard work. God used to walk each day in the garden and visit with Adam and Eve, but sin changed that. "Then to Adam He said, 'Because you have heeded the voice of your wife and have eaten from the tree of which I commanded you, saying, 'You shall not eat of it': Cursed *is* the ground for your sake; In toil you shall eat *of* it All the days of your life. Both thorns and thistles it shall bring forth for you'...therefore the LORD God sent him out of the garden of Eden to till the ground from which he was taken." Genesis 3:17, 18, 23 (NKJV).

The Beginning of Tilling the Soil

Paul Gautschi noticed that, when sin came into the picture, man now had to till the ground to make it productive. He considered the fact that the surface of the earth is not exposed unless man tills or disturbs it. He noted that the ground is a living organism, and just like man has skin, and animals have fur, the ground in its natural state has a covering as well. When man removes that protective layer, the soil becomes vulnerable.

Pruning

Jesus said, "I am the true vine, and My Father is the vinedresser. Every branch in Me that does not bear fruit He takes away; and every *branch* that bears fruit He prunes, that it may bear more fruit." John 15:1, 2 (NKJV). After reading this verse, Paul realized that to bear more fruit, a gardener needs to not only cut off a branch that does not bear fruit but prune those that do, so the tree can produce more fruit.

Sustainable Permaculture

Paul has mentioned to people who have visited his garden to remember "sustainable permaculture". According to Paul, sustainable means "conserving and ecological balance by avoiding depletion of natural resources" and permaculture means "the development of an agricultural system or method intended to be sustainable and self-sufficient." (Back to Eden, 2022).

Soil Benefits

As stated in the description of the *Back to Eden* documentary film, "Back to Eden Gardening is a regenerative agriculture method since it rebuilds soil and restores soil biodiversity resulting in both carbon drawdown and improving the water cycle." (Back to Eden, 2022). It is therefore suggested that using this approach to gardening can help rebuild and restore the soil from its depleted condition to a vibrant, healthy earth.

Water Benefits

This method claims to also help with the issue of water and the need for irrigation. Paul's experience has been that by properly applying the mulch wood chips year after year, there is little or no need to water the trees, even during a drought. This results in creating a more balanced water cycle.

Gardening Poor Soil

Paul's Back to Eden method of gardening has spawned a revolution around the world. Paul showed how he planted on hard dirt as well as on a bed of rocks. The *Back to Eden* documentary film shows examples of people planting gardens on lawns or even on concrete!

The Base

The Back to Eden website explains that the layers would be on top of the undisturbed ground, starting with newspaper. Why newspaper? It would suffocate the weeds below while allowing moisture through. Over time the paper would decompose resulting in the continuous connection of the added layers to the virgin soil.

Seed Start image used with permission from Back to Eden

Compost Layer

The next layer would be compost. According to the US Composting Council, compost "is the product manufactured through the controlled aerobic, biological decomposition of biodegradable materials. The product has undergone mesophilic and thermophilic temperatures, which significantly reduces the viability of pathogens and weed seeds … and stabilizes the carbon such that it is beneficial to plant growth." (US Composting Council, 2023).

Wood Chips Layer

According to Leaf & Limb, "Instead of being heavily processed hardwood, wood chips are simply large chunks of tree branches and trunks that are the byproduct of pruning trees. It is a cleaner mulch that provides more benefits to your trees and shrubs." The benefits are that it "feeds the soil…regulates temperature…regulates moisture…reduces waste…free and ready to use…suppresses weeds." (Camu, 2020).

Plant Start image used with permission from Back to Eden

Manure Layer

The final layer in the Back to Eden method is manure. Cow manure is preferred over horse manure. "Sometimes you can find a farmer willing to sell a load of cow manure from a barn mixed with straw. If offered this, then, by all means, accept as it can be used as the basis of a hot compost heap, a hotbed or just covered over to rot down for a few months before applying." (Harrison, 2023).

Based on the various successes seen by people using the Back to Eden method of gardening, this approach would be worth considering when planning your sustainable country garden. Keep in mind, if you just dump raw wood chips in your garden, you will be disappointed in the results. Watch the *Back to Eden* documentary film online to learn more and to carefully plan how you might choose to use this approach in your country garden.

References

Bible. The New King James Version, 2020, Genesis 3:17, 18, 23.

Bible. The New King James Version, 2020, John 15:1, 2.

Back to Eden. (2022). *Back to Eden Gardening Documentary*. Retrieved September 19, 2023, from https://www.backtoedenfilm.com/watchfreeorgani cgardeningmovie.html#/.

US Composting Council. (2023). *Compost Definition - Composting Council*. Compost Definition. https://www.compostingcouncil.org/page/Compost Definition

Camu, B. (2020, September 20). *Top 10 Reasons to Choose Wood Chips Over Other Types of Mulch*. Ten Top Reasons to Choose Wood Chips. https://www.leaflimb.com/Top-Ten-Reasons-to-Choose-Wood-Chips/

Harrison, V. (2023) *Horse or Cow Manure - Which is Better?*. Allotment & Gardens. https://www.allotment-garden.org/composts-fertilisers/horse-or-cow-manure/

Watch the Back to Eden Documentary Online

https://www.backtoedenfilm.com/watchfreeorganicgarde ningmovie.html

Chapter 27: Food Grid – Gardening: Mittleider Method

Jacob Mittleider, a Seventh-day Adventist, became known around the world for his gardening method. He was an international agricultural consultant as well as conducting humanitarian training projects. This was based on his over fifty years of wholesale plant production and gardening experience. In 1964 Loma Linda University asked him to travel the world to understand the nutritional needs of developing countries including Africa, India, the Middle East, and the countries of the Pacific Rim. His findings resulted in recommendations regarding methods of growing nutritious produce to help these regions with malnutrition solutions through his high-yield growing principles and procedures.

Garden image used with permission from Food for
Everyone Foundation

Jacob Mittleider's Impact

"The economies of countries as diverse and far flung as
Papua New Guinea, Trinidad & Tobago, and Russia were
changed forever by the knowledge their growers received
from this uniquely skilled and dedicated man. Whenever he
was not actually conducting an agriculture training program
somewhere Jacob was diligently working on documenting
everything he did by writing 10 gardening books and
producing 86 slide-show lectures. Over the years Jacob
Mittleider was recognized and honored by universities on
four continents, even receiving an honorary PhD from the
most prestigious agricultural university in the Soviet
Union." (FFEF, 2023).

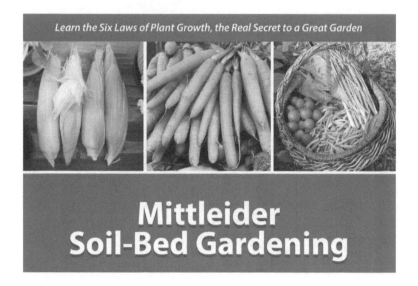

Mittleider image used with permission from Food for Everyone Foundation

Jim Kennard

Jim Kennard lived in Salt Lake City, Utah. In the 70's the Church of Jesus Christ of Latter-day Saints leaders encouraged members to be prepared for difficult times by being self-sustaining. As a result, Jim expanded his gardening passion to include the techniques he found in Jacob Mittleider's book *More Food from Your Garden*, resulting in him being able to feed his family fresh produce for half of the year from a small 20 x 30 garden space.

Kennard and Mittleider Collaborate

In 1976, Jim was excited to find that Jacob Mittleider moved from Loma Linda, CA to within a mile of Jim's home in Salt Lake City! They became fast friends, with Jim and Jacob working together on several projects including a month-long project in Russia. In 1998, he asked Jim to take over his materials and continue his legacy by making his *Mittleider Method* books and training materials available long after his passing. Until the death of Jacob Mittleider in 2006 at the age of 86, Jim Kennard continued to consult with Jacob as Jim conducted humanitarian gardening training projects of his own in several countries.

The Mittleider Method

The Mittleider Method uses soil-based gardening with feeding of a balanced supply of natural mineral nutrients much like is done with hydroponics, but without the need for hydroponics equipment. These crops are high yield because plant spacings are done very close together (based on size at maturity), minimizing weeds and greatly increasing productivity. This method can be done in the native soil, with no soil amendments, but also often utilizes above-ground containers filled with sawdust and concrete sand. Using the Mittleider Method promises to be able to raise a large portion of the family's food needs from a gardening space as small as 1/20th of an acre.

Plants in Close Proximity

This approach to gardening has the plants near each other, two rows of plants in an 18" wide bed, with wide aisles, rather than in single rows with more space between them. The result is a high yield of produce in a very small space. To make up for the possible lack of nutrients due to the concentration of plants, these necessary components are supplied by the regular application of very small amounts of balanced natural mineral nutrients to the soil.

Limited Space Gardening

The Mittleider Method utilizes a minimal amount of space to produce a substantial quantity of vegetation, therefore it is ideal for those with limited available gardening space such as in a city. Some even use this method when living in an apartment and growing in planters on a deck, a patio, or even a flat roof or driveway. As explained by backyardville.com, grow beds are more beginner-friendly, require less work up front, are less expensive to construct, and only require simple gardening tools. They also explained that grow boxes (as compared to grow beds) "can be built almost anywhere; even on a parking lot" and are almost weedless. (Thomas, 2017).

World Food Production Problems

As stated in Mittleider's own words, "... almost constant study, research, and field application on food production problems in many parts of the world have long since convinced me that the most promising approach is a synthesis of the best features of several major methods of gardening. Organic gardening emphasizes plant access to all available soil nutrients and microbial activity; conventional gardening emphasizes adequate fertilization and pest control; hydroponic gardening emphasizes high-density planting in a controlled environment. But each of these methods, alone, has some limitations. What I have been teaching and demonstrating in various countries is a bringing together of the best scientific knowledge and experience in each of these approaches. I believe that the results speak for themselves." (Mittleider, 2018).

Garden image used with permission from Food for Everyone Foundation

Light

The Mittleider Method of gardening capitalizes on the six laws of plant growth. While few gardeners seem to completely understand these principles, they are laws of nature, therefore, are unchangeable and immutable, according to Mittleider. The first of these laws is light. Light is essential to plant growth utilizing photosynthesis. Plants do their best with as much light as possible for as long as possible during the day. Six to eight hours of direct daily sunlight is the minimum needed for ideal productivity for most vegetables.

Temperature

The second law of plant growth is temperature. Most plants need soils of 70-85°F for ideal seed germination, while outdoor plants do best with 60-90°F for plant growth and production.

Air

Air is the third law of plant growth. According to Mittleider, plants gain three nutrients from the atmosphere: carbon, oxygen, and hydrogen. These combined allow the plant to create carbohydrates.

Water

Water is the fourth law of plant growth, with plants being mostly made up of water. The plant's root system must have the right amount of water for the plant to survive and be productive.

Nutrition

The fifth law for plants is nutrition. Mittleider identified 16 nutrients essential for plant growth and productivity. The atmosphere provides carbon, oxygen, and hydrogen, while the others are macro-nutrients nitrogen, phosphorus, and potassium, secondary nutrients calcium, magnesium, and sulfur, and 7 trace elements, zinc, boron, manganese, iron, copper, chloride, and molybdenum. For plants to thrive, they need a balance of all 16 nutrients.

Protection

The last need for plants is identified as "law" number six, which is protecting plants from unwanted competition. This rivalry with the plant can be from weeds, pests, animals, or disease.

Available Course

Jacob Mittleider and Jim Kennard collaborated on a step-by-step short course on how to use the Mittleider Method, which is available in a downloadable PDF document format. The lessons are broken into seven topics: planning, preparing, planting, watering, fertilizing, weeding, and harvesting, in both soil beds and containers or Grow-Boxes. There are also 10 lessons on advanced topics and four excellent appendixes. The book includes 150 full-color pictures of great gardens and dozens of professional illustrations of all the gardening processes. Included is Dr. Mittleider's Gardening Cycle Calendar, which explains what to do for each month of the year.

Edible Parts of Plants

Also included in the downloadable document is a list of edible parts of vegetable plants and what times of the year to harvest each of the different types of vegetables. The

Mittleider Gardening Method promises to maximize space, time, and resources in a high-yield garden space. It takes the guesswork out of gardening and makes it possible to grow a garden almost anywhere.

References:

FFEF (2023). *Food For Everyone Foundation*. Foundation
     Blog RSS. https://growfood.com/meet-dr-mittledier/

Thomas, N. (2017, February 23). *The Mittleider Gardening
     Method: Answers to all of your questions*.
     Backyardville. https://backyardville.com/mittleider-
     gardening-method/

Mittleider, J. (2018). *Mittleider Soil-Bed Gardening*.
     https://growfood.com/wp-
     content/uploads/2018/12/Mittleider_Soil_Bed_Gard
     ening_v5_download.pdf

Additional Resources:

Free short course, including the first 7 Lessons of the
Mittleider Gardening Course in downloadable PDF form:

https://growfood.com/wp-
content/uploads/2018/12/Mittleider_Soil_Bed_Gardening
_v5_download.pdf

The complete 304-page Mittleider Gardening Course book
is also available - in print or downloadable - at
https://growfood.com/shop/the-mittleider-gardening-
course/

Chapter 28: Food Grid – Gardening: Ellen White Method

Lynn Hoag spent time as a child living in India with missionary parents. There he saw families lacking enough food and thus developed an interest in growing food. After his parents returned to the U.S. when he was 13 years of age, he participated in a gardening class taught by Herbert Clarence White, a grandson of Ellen White.

Amazing Results

Lynn Hoag explained, "The Ellen White growing method is so amazing you almost have to see it to believe it. At one of my garden classes, someone suggested we plant some trees with the regular method and one with the Ellen White method and see what happens. We planted five sequoias the forestry department method and one the Ellen White method. As you can see in the picture the one on my right is much larger and stronger. This is no trick. We planted 6 trees the same size on the same day and in the same location." (Hoag, 2020).

Planting the Ellen White Method image used with permission from Lynn Hoag

A Planting Revelation

Over 100 years ago, Ellen White had been sent to Australia as a missionary with the intention to start a Christian school. She believed that God had revealed to her in a dream what the school property would look like. She was part of a group of people looking for the location for the future school. Several properties were passed up during the search because they were not suitable or too expensive. Then they came across one piece of land that did not look promising because the soil was not good for agriculture. But Ellen recognized the features of the property from the dream. She knew God had directed them to that location for the new school.

Passing on the Legacy

Ellen White was shown in a dream how to treat unsuitable land to make it productive. And fruitful it was! Even though Ellen never wrote down the formula for this method of gardening, later her grandson Herbert Clarence White assisted Ellen in person implementing the method. So, it was passed down from generation to generation. When Lynn Hoag, at the age of 13, took Herbert's hands-on class, he realized that this system was something that needed to be made available to others. Even since that time, Lynn has been using this method, and much of his life is dedicated to helping others learn this amazing gardening method. The Ellen White method, as it has become known, not only works well growing fruit trees but any plant with deep roots such as tomatoes, grapes, and kiwi. In some cases, the yield increases by 300%.

Ellen White Planting Method

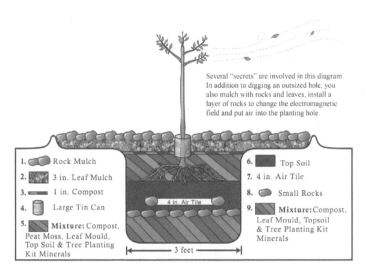

Several "secrets" are involved in this diagram. In addition to digging an outsized hole, you also mulch with rocks and leaves, install a layer of rocks to change the electromagnetic field and put air into the planting hole.

1. Rock Mulch
2. 3 in. Leaf Mulch
3. 1 in. Compost
4. Large Tin Can
5. Mixture: Compost, Peat Moss, Leaf Mould, Top Soil & Tree Planting Kit Minerals
6. Top Soil
7. 4 in. Air Tile
8. Small Rocks
9. Mixture: Compost, Leaf Mould, Topsoil & Tree Planting Kit Minerals

4 in. Air Tile

3 feet

Ellen White Planting Method Cutaway image used with permission from Lynn Hoag

The Method

While some people over the years have made modifications and enhancements to the Ellen White method, the core components remain consistent. This process involves digging a hole three feet wide and three feet deep. That is a very big hole to dig by hand, so using a backhoe or mini-excavator would be desirable if planting more than one tree at a time. The hole is filled with layers of different components. The bottom third of the hole is filled with a mixture of compost, leaf mold, topsoil, and five pounds of phosphate rock or colloidal phosphate. Next, a layer of small rocks is placed in the hole.

Modern Modifications

One modern modification is to lay a 4-inch PVC pipe to trap air or water underground. The ends of the pipe are capped with one rock on each end. Next a layer about a foot thick is filled with topsoil. Now put into the center of the hole a large stone. The roots of the new tree are positioned around the stone. The remaining hole is filled to the top with a mixture of compost, peat moss, leaf mold, topsoil, and minerals. The lower stock of the plant is protected from rodent damage with a large tin can or hardware cloth surrounding the tree trunk. Now that the hole is filled, the area on top of the hole and the surrounding area is covered with leaf mulch. Finally, optionally, above the mulch can be a layer of small rocks.

Documented Success

While Ellen White did not write down the instructions for planting this method, she did document the results, "Our crops were very successful. The peaches were beautiful in coloring, and the most delicious in flavor of any that I had tasted. We grew the large yellow Crawford and other varieties, grapes, apricots, nectarines, and plums." (White, 1980).

Growing Tomatoes

There was an experiment made in the past called The Tomato Project where the Ellen White method was applied to growing tomatoes. Commercial tomato project operations typically yield 15-35 tons per acre. This works out to be about 5-12 lbs. of harvestable tomatoes per plant. Long-season tomato plants in greenhouses can double this yield from 10-25 lbs. per plant. The Tomato Project showed that tomatoes grown using the Ellen White method consistently yielded 100 pounds per plant for large-sized varieties!

Ocean Water

Lynn Hoag also explains that all ocean water has the same components around the world, and interestingly similar to human blood. Lynn uses ocean water as an additive for fruit trees each spring. It is particularly helpful in combating peach leaf curl, which is an uncontrolled growth of cells, caused by a virus. The ocean water mixture would be one quart of ocean water to five quarts of water. He sprays the diluted ocean water onto the leaves as well as pours it on the ground for the roots to absorb.

Treating Diseased Leaves

For a leaf that is half diseased and half healthy, the result will be the diseased part will die and the healthy part will become healthier. The minerals in the ocean water that were spread on the ground and absorbed by the roots, result in not only a healthier tree as well as more attractive fruit with a sweeter flavor. With a healthy tree, he suggests each spring placing a mixture of one quart of ocean water to ten quarts of water around the base of the tree.

The Ellen White method has been utilized by many people over the years and has proven to be a worthwhile effort to have a yield of healthy rooted trees and plants.

References

Hoag, L. (2020) *Sun Country Gardens - healing gardening.* Sun Country Gardens - Healing Gardening. https://www.suncountrygardens.com/

White, E. G. (1980). *Selected Messages* (Vol. 3). Review and Herald Publishing Association.

Additional Video and Podcast Resources

www.preparingforthetimeoftrouble.com- Part 22 "Planting the Ellen White Method"

Audio Recordings of Lynn Hoag's Classes

https://www.audioverse.org/en/presenters/966/lynn-hoag

Chapter 29: Food Grid – Gardening: Seed Saving

Saving seeds is very important for long-term sustainable gardening. While a person can now easily purchase seeds at a store or online, there may come a time when this could be difficult. It is therefore important to understand the difference between open-pollinated and hybrid plants.

Open-Pollinated and Hybrid

You need to establish whether a plant is a hybrid or open-pollinated variety. Seeds saved from open-pollinated plants will be identical to the parent plant. Hybrids on the other hand do not have the same traits as the parent plant.

Seed Starts image used with permission from Kellogg Garden Products

Heirloom Seeds

Harvested seeds should be open-pollinated. Some call these "heritage" seeds, while others may call them "heirloom" seeds. According to the University of Minnesota Extension, "Open-pollinated varieties may be heirlooms. These varieties may be passed down through generations." (UNM, 2018). They go on to identify that tomatoes, beans, peas, and peppers are particularly good for seed saving.

Purchasing Seeds

Open-pollinated seeds are preferred. When a person buys seeds, many times they are a hybrid variety, meaning it has been crossed by different varieties of plants. The problem is that if you were to save the seeds from that plant, the tendency would be for the next generation of plants to not have the same traits as the parent plant.

Selecting Seeds

As you can see there can be multiple reasons why it would be good to carefully plan to collect seeds that can be replicated year after year. The key point is that you should purchase open-pollinated seeds and avoid hybrid seeds, which are often the types you would buy at a store. Organic plants have not been sprayed with chemicals. Some market gardeners practice organic methods but have not gone through the process of becoming certified as organic farmers.

Sources of Seeds

There are many good sources for open-pollinated seeds through catalogs and online such as Seed Savers Exchange, Johnny's Selected Seeds, High Mowing, and Baker Creek. Seed Savers Exchange explains, "So what are open-pollinated varieties, and what is their lifespan? Open-pollinated varieties are like dog breeds; they will retain their distinct characteristics as long as they are mated with the same breed. This means, with a little care and planning, the seeds you produce will be true-to-type, keeping their distinct traits generation after generation as long as they do not cross-pollinate with other varieties of the same species." (SeedSavers, 2023). Seed Savers Exchange offers online videos of how to process tomato, squash, pepper, legumes, and watermelon seeds (see link below).

Good Seed Sources

A farmer's market would be a good place to do some research to find a source for produce that has not been affected by spraying. One person has been able to purchase produce from Amish or Mennonite farmers. These usually follow organic growing practices, and the saved seeds have an almost 100% germination rate.

Patented Seeds

According to journalist Tove Danovich, "Beginning with the 1970 Plant Variety Protection Act (PVPA), which granted companies a certificate ownership of seeds, and the 1980 Supreme Court case *Diamond v. Chakrabarty,* which allowed seeds full patent protection, seed ownership began to look more like intellectual property law. In many cases, farmers were no longer allowed to save seeds and breeders couldn't use patented seeds to breed new plant varieties either. Today, the bulk of seed breeding has moved from public universities to private laboratories and four companies control more than 60 percent of global seed sales." (Danovich, 2020).

Being Self-Sustaining

One very important reason to collect seeds is to be able to be self-sustaining during difficult times. This could be when the supply of seeds has been hampered, either by supply and demand issues or intentionally by large seed companies controlling availability. What if conditions got bad enough that you could not buy or sell at all? It would be good in any of these scenarios to have planned ahead and been in the practice of collecting seeds.

Seed Saving image used with permission from Kellogg Garden Products

Easy to Collect Seeds

Not all seeds are harvested and stored the same. If you are a beginner, here are some of the easier plants from which to collect seeds. Tomatoes, peppers, beans and peas are a good place to start. On the other hand, there are some vegetables that are more complicated to collect seeds. For instance, carrots and beets are biennial crops. This means it takes two seasons to produce seeds. No matter which variety of plant you are collecting seeds, you should select the healthiest plant with the best fruit from which to collect the seeds.

Different Ways to Harvest Seeds

There are differing opinions about the best way to harvest and store seeds, so a person should do some research for each type of seed because not all seeds should be processed in the same way. For instance, Iowa State University Extension explains, "Seeds from flesh fruit, such as peppers and pumpkins, should be collected when the fruit is completely ripe and even over ripe and starting to shrivel on the plant. Scoop the seeds out and separate from the gel or pulp, rinse them off and lay them out on paper towels to thoroughly dry. Seeds that aren't completely dried may mold while in storage." (Naeve, 1970

Harvesting Seeds

Jessica Sowards suggests, "Root vegetables and greenery need to be allowed to bolt so that you can collect the seeds. This is how you'll save the seeds from carrots, radishes, beets, lettuces, broccoli, and even some flowers." (Sowards, 2021). Kidsgardening.org offers an online, downloadable chart for kids learning to save seeds showing which type to save, when to save them, and how to collect them (see link below).

Saved Seeds image used with permission from Kellogg Garden Products

Seed Saving Resource

We have been introduced to harvesting seeds for some plants. It is important to do research for each kind of fruit or vegetable that you want to seed save. There are many good resources on the Internet and YouTube videos for learning how to collect seeds. One online resource is growveg.org which has information about saving seeds.

Storing Seeds

Linda Naeve provides a recommendation about the proper storage of the seeds. "Seeds are living organisms and if they are stored improperly, they will lose their viability. They should be stored dry in a cool location, and preferably in an air tight container. Put the seeds in a small paper envelope or wrap in paper. Label the envelope with the name of the plant and the date you collected the seed. Place the envelopes in a glass jar or air tight plastic container. To keep the seed dry, it is a good idea to put a desiccant in the jar to absorb moisture from the air. Silica gel that is sold in bulk for drying flowers can be used or the small packets of desiccants often found in shoe boxes. A tablespoon or two of powdered milk wrapped in a facial tissue and placed in the seed storage container will also work to absorb excess moisture from the air. Seal the container and store it in the back of your refrigerator." (Naeve, 1970).

Fun and Life Saving Hobby

Seed saving can be a fun hobby but more importantly, it is a very critical part of being sustainable. Having a perpetual system of collecting seeds can ensure that you can replicate your favorite plants from year to year without having to depend on outside sources for seeds. This is not only an important benefit for your gardening efforts but may be a lifesaver!

References

Danovich, T. (2020, April 21). *Gardening is important, but seed saving is crucial*. Civil Eats. https://civileats.com/2020/04/21/gardening-is-important-but-seed-saving-is-crucial/

UMN. (2018). *Saving vegetable seeds*. UMN Extension. https://extension.umn.edu/planting-and-growing-guides/saving-vegetable-seeds

SeedSavers. (2023, September 13). *Seed saving*. https://seedsavers.org/learn/seed-saving/

Sowards, J. (2021, December 15). *A complete guide to seed saving*. Roots and Refuge. https://rootsandrefuge.com/a-complete-guide-to-seed-saving/

Naeve, L. (1970, September 1). *Saving seeds from your garden*. Small Farm Sustainability. https://www.extension.iastate.edu/smallfarms/saving-seeds-your-garden

Additional Video and Podcast Resources

www.preparingforthetimeoftrouble.com - Part 20
"Seed Saving When You Can't Buy or Sell"

Recommended Seed Catalogs

Baker Creek Heirloom Seeds - www.rareseeds.com

High Mowing Organic Seeds - www.highmowingseeds.com

Johnny's Selected Seeds - www.johnnyseeds.com

Seed Savers Exchange – www.seedsavers.org

West Coast Seeds - www.westcoastseeds.com

Additional Resources

https://seedsavers.org/learn/seed-saving/

https://kidsgardening.org/wp-content/uploads/2018/08/Seed-Saving-Chart.pdf

Chapter 30: Food Grid – Gardening: Extended Season

Unless you live near the equator, you are typically unable to grow food year-round. Of course, there are some vegetables that can grow outdoors during the winter in some parts of the country, but most cannot during the cold temperatures of the year. This results in a window of time during the year when the gardens are most productive. Fortunately, there are some strategies one can use to stretch the growing season, resulting in starting the season earlier and lasting longer. In this chapter, we will investigate several things you can build that will help do just that.

Season Extenders

The key element needed to extend a growing season is to protect the plants with some form of a covering. These can include a cold frame which is usually small, a hoop house which is big enough to walk and work inside, a greenhouse which is similar but more permanent and durable, and lastly, a high tunnel, which is large enough to drive equipment inside. Which of these approaches to use depends on the size of the gardening effort and the funds available. We will discuss each of these so you will understand which might fit your budget and needs.

Cold Frame

A cold frame is a box that is made much like a raised bed but has a removable glass top to allow the air in the enclosed space to stay warmer and capitalize on the sun when it is shining through the glass. While there are commercially made cold frames available, most of the time the gardener simply constructs their own, even using used or left-over materials. A tour of YouTube videos would result in a treasure trove of ideas from those who made their own.

Home-Made Cold Frame

A cold frame can be built by using boards to create a box with a slanted upper edge. If a person has an acrylic top or old window frame, the box could be built to match the size of the window frame and fasten the window on the top side with a pair of hinges. This will allow the owner to manually open and close the lid as needed. Some have used an automatic opener which does not require electricity. It is a cylinder with a wax piston inside. The wax contracts or expands based on the heat. One such device is the Bayliss Auto Vent Opener available from acfgreenhouses.com.

The Box

The box is like a raised bed, making it easier to grow plants if the inside soil is higher than the surrounding ground. The opening lid makes access to the plants easy. The lid can be closed to allow the sun to warm up the area through the glass, and trap that warm air resulting in an overall warmer plant-growing environment. This would be especially helpful during cool evenings because the lid would keep out the colder air. This combination of benefits makes a cold frame an inexpensive, easy-to-build addition to your garden to extend the growing season for the plants inside.

Protected Growing Space

For those who want larger areas protected from the elements, there are three additional options. RIMOL Greenhouses explains it this way, "Whether you're a professional farmer looking to extend your growing season and improve your annual output, or simply a backyard gardener looking to take your veggies to the next level, a protected growing space can really make a difference - but when it comes to making the right choice, you've got options. Generally, today's farmers interested in choosing from the wide variety of protected growing spaces available have three main options to choose from: high tunnels, greenhouses, and hoop houses." (RIMOL, 2023).

High Tunnels

High tunnels are mostly used by farmers as compared to home gardeners. This is because a high tunnel is designed to work the soil at ground level within the structure and has a high enough ceiling to accommodate a tractor or other equipment to work inside the building. These kinds of structures are semi-permanent but can be disassembled and moved if needed. More often, the outer film can be removed during the heat of the summer, to allow full sun to reach the crop inside, leaving the framework in place. Because of the size and expense involved, a high tunnel is rarely used by the home gardener.

Greenhouses

According to RIMOL Greenhouses, "A true traditional greenhouse is a grow space designed for full-year operation—providing protection that often exceeds that offered by a high tunnel or hoop house." (RIMOL, 2023). One significant difference between a high tunnel and a greenhouse is that a high tunnel would not have any raised beds, while some greenhouse owners like to have raised beds and even layered shelves to allow for easier working of the plant space by the gardener. A greenhouse is designed to be a permanent structure, therefore the transparent panels typically are either glass or polycarbonate. To further control the cold temperatures out of the greenhouse, many times polycarbonate sheeting is multi-layered. There are differing thicknesses of air space available between the polycarbonate layers. The larger the air space, the more insulation value. While a creative gardener can build their greenhouse, often, a greenhouse is commercially made and professionally installed or comes as a kit.

Greenhouse by B.C. Greenhouse Builders

Greenhouses can be free-standing or in the form of a lean-to taking advantage of a wall of a building. An advantage of the lean-to style is that the adjacent wall would be warmer than having a greenhouse exterior wall on the shaded side of the greenhouse. Some greenhouse builders may choose to add some heat adsorbing and retaining function by including some black water tanks or a wall of rockwork on the back side of the greenhouse. This allows for the heat of the sun to be captured by the mass and stored there, radiating it later in the evening and night to passively raise the greenhouse temperature when the sun is gone.

Greenhouse by B.C. Greenhouse Builders

Hoop Houses

Hoop houses are the next method to be able to extend your garden growing season. "A hoop house is a DIY greenhouse that sits in your garden. You can build it by using cattle fencing or PVC hoops wrapped in plastic covering. You can either build your hoop house in a raised bed, or as a row cover in your current garden bed." (FPS, 2023).

Three Ways to Construct a Hoop House

Hoop houses can be made at least three ways. The arched roof supports can be made with EMT electrical conduit bent in a homemade jig. Another approach is to use PVC plastic pipe, which is easy to work with and will bend without any effort. Lastly, a person can use cattle panels from a farm store. Rather than using them laterally as a fence, the hoop house would have the cattle panel end secured to the ground and then bent to make the arch and secure the other end to the ground.

Beating the Heat

Whether you have a hoop house or a greenhouse, there may be times in the heat of summer when the plants need protection from direct sunlight. This can be accomplished with a product called "shade cloth". There are many sources to purchase this, but a good place to start is a greenhouse supply store. Shade cloth can be ordered in different percentages of blockage so consult with the company selling the cloth to have them recommend what percentage of blockage is best for your situation.

Online Resources

The Internet and YouTube have numerous sets of instructions for a variety of approaches to creating easy-to-build, affordable hoop houses or cold frames. Either of these approaches is a great way to create your first covered garden space to be able to extend your growing season. Incorporating a cold frame, hoop house, greenhouse, or high tunnel can add a long-lasting dimension to the gardening capabilities.

References

RIMOL. (2023). *High tunnel vs. Greenhouse vs. Hoop House: Which is right for me?* https://rimol.com/blog/high-tunnel-vs-greenhouse-vs-hoop-house-which-is-right-for-me-8adea9/

FPS. (2023). *How to build a Hoop House greenhouse.* https://farmplasticsupply.com/blog/how-to-build-a-hoop-house-greenhouse

Additional Video and Podcast Resources

www.preparingforthetimeoftrouble.com - Part 26 "Extending the Garden Growing Season with Cold Frames, Hoop Houses, and Greenhouses"

www.preparingforthetimeoftrouble.com – Part 343 "Bending Metal Pipe to Build a Hoop House"

Chapter 30: Food Grid – Gardening: Extended Season

Chapter 31: Food Grid – Garden Produce Preservation

It is possible to eat fresh food from your garden most of the summer. Unless you live near the equator, your garden will not produce all year. Therefore, it will be necessary to preserve your food for the off-season. Depending on the type of produce you are attempting to save for later, there are several methods that can be used to preserve food.

The main purpose of food preservation is to keep food from spoiling, avoid food poisoning, prevent microbial contamination, and kill any pathogens. Without these important precautions, people could get very sick and possibly die from food poisoning. The Home and Garden Information Center states that "Food preservation involves slowing down or stopping the natural processes that cause food to spoil, such as oxidation, bacterial growth, and enzymatic activity. There are several methods of food preservation, each with its own advantages and disadvantages, and it is important to choose the right one for your specific needs." (Yebba, 2023).

Eva Maria Hanson, a food safety specialist, states, "For every food preservation method to become successful, proper sanitation and hygiene must also be present. Without proper sanitation, even the strictest methods of preservation, such as canning, can become harmful to consumers." (Hanson, 2023).

Canned Food image source: Pixabay

Dehydrating and Sun Drying

The University of Missouri Extension published an article explaining that "Foods can be dehydrated by various means: the sun, a conventional oven, an electric dehydrator, a microwave oven (for herbs only), air drying and solar drying.

Dehydration, like other preservation methods, requires energy. Unless sun drying is possible where you live, the energy cost of dehydrating foods at home is higher than for canning and, in some cases, more expensive than freezing." (Willienberg, 2023).

Freeze Drying

Mill Rock Technology explains that freeze drying, "is a water removal process typically used to preserve perishable materials, with the goal of extending their shelf life and/or preparing them for transport. Freeze drying works by freezing the material, then reducing the pressure and adding heat to allow the frozen water in the material to change directly to a vapor". (Millrock, 2023).

Freezing

Many prefer freezing food for preserving. Advantages include ease of processing, fresher taste, and retention of coloring. Disadvantages could be a lack of freezer space available and possible food loss in the event of a power failure. Also, if a person is off-grid, power consumption for operating a freezer needs to be an important consideration. Fruit can be frozen fresh while vegetables will need to be blanched before freezing. Freezing can be done by cooling the food and wrapping it in sealed plastic bags or containers. These should be in manageable-sized portions, identified by date to be able to rotate stock.

Canning - Water Bath

Water bath canning is the method used for generations to preserve food in canning jars. While it is a very good method for canning some garden produce, it is only appropriate for acidic foods such as fruit. This method cannot be safely used for low-acid foods such as potatoes, pumpkins, and meat. It is important to follow instructions carefully when water bath canning to ensure safety during the process and success with the final product. One source for trusted instructions is in the Ball Blue Book, produced by the makers of Ball canning jars.

Canning – Steam Canning

Steam canning is like water bath canning, but uses steam rather than hot water, consequently, it takes less water to heat, resulting in a quicker processing time. Like water bath canning, this method is good for naturally acid and acidified foods. This process is quick and simple but be sure to use appropriate equipment and processes to ensure safety and successful final products.

Canning – Pressure Canning

Older pressure canners were heavy-walled kettles with clamp-on or turn-on lids. These were cumbersome and, in some cases, dangerous. Modern pressure canners are lighter-weight and come with removable racks, a gauge, and a safety valve. They are deep enough for a layer of quart canning jars. There can be some dangerous errors in operation so be sure to follow the manufacturer's instructions carefully to ensure safety. Pressure canning can be used to preserve green beans, tomato juice, salsa, corn, onions, squash, and potatoes.

Fermentation

When we hear the term fermentation, most of us think of alcohol such as beer or wine, but fermentation is actually a viable option for preserving food. Fermentation is the chemical process of converting sugars to ethanol. Fermented food can be a good source for beneficial bacteria and helps to make available some nutrients. Some examples of fermented foods are yogurt, cheese, pickles, sourdough bread, and sauerkraut.

Pickling

The pickling process of food preservation uses an acidic brine made with salt, sugar, lemon juice, or vinegar. Pickling is done by pouring the brine over the fruits or vegetables and then storing them in jars for a few days. The most common type of pickled food is pickled cucumbers or pickles. Other foods can be pickled, from carrots to radishes, to hard-boiled eggs. Commercially produced pickles found on the grocery store shelf are water-bath canned, which kills bacteria and makes them shelf-stable. By comparison, homemade, refrigerated pickled foods, are not heat-processed so need to be kept cold in a refrigerator for up to a month.

Juicing

Fruit juice is another preservation method. A couple of ways it can be done are by steaming or by squeezing the fruit, such as when making apple cider in a cider press. A canning process would then be used to make the juice ready for storing such as water bath canning. Juicing can be successfully done with almost any type of fruit. The length of shelf-life depends on the acid level of the juice, how the jars are stored, and the type of juicer used. Glass jars are the preferred container to be used to store the juice.

Salting

Using salt to preserve food is mostly used with processing meat and fish. To use salt as a preservative, the percentage of salt by weight would be very large, such as 15 percent. From a sustainable perspective, using salt as a preservative would not be practical because of the need for such a large quantity of salt needed.

Summer Kitchen

One passing thought has to do with water-bath canning or other methods requiring heat. Harvesting is usually at the end of summer and into the fall. Canning over a hot stove can be complicated with it potentially being a hot day when you need to can. If you are in a sustainable situation and depending on a wood stove for cooking, this could multiply the issue of the kitchen being very hot and uncomfortable. In that case, one could resort to a time-tested, old-fashioned approach. An outdoor summer kitchen is a food processing area that is outside rather than in the home kitchen. By having a wood-burning kitchen stove on a covered porch, canning can be done with a wood stove on a hot day in a much more comfortable environment than would be in a home kitchen.

Options

As you can see from this brief overview of different options for preserving garden produce, there are different approaches that can be taken depending on which food is being processed and the equipment available.

References

Yebba, A., (2023). *Preserving freshness: The Basics of Food Preservation*. Home & Garden Information Center | Clemson University, South Carolina. https://hgic.clemson.edu/preserving-freshness-the-basics-of-food-preservation/

Hanson, E. M. (2023). *What is food preservation and how to do it properly?*. What is Food Preservation and how to do it Properly? https://www.fooddocs.com/post/food-preservation

Willienberg, B., & Mills-Gray, S. (2023.). *Introduction to food dehydration*. University of Missouri Extension. https://extension.missouri.edu/publications/gh1562

Millrock. (2023). *What is freeze drying? how does it work? Millrock Technology, Inc.*. Millrock Technology, Inc. https://www.millrocktech.com/lyosight/lyobrary/what-is-freeze-drying/

Additional Video and Podcast Resources

www.preparingforthetimeoftrouble.com – Part 27
"Preserving Food by Canning When You Can't Buy or Sell"

www.preparingforthetimeoftrouble.com – Part 37
"Emergency and Long-Term Food Storage"

www.preparingforthetimeoftrouble.com – Part 42
"Drying Food When You Can't Buy or Sell"

www.preparingforthetimeoftrouble.com – Part 74
"Pantries and Cold Rooms"

www.preparingforthetimeoftrouble.com – Part 189
"Storing Food Without Electricity"

Chapter 32: What to Look for in Country Property

In his book *Strategic Relocation*, Joel Skousen identifies what types of property to look for, "We recommend forested, mountain or hill country areas for retreats and lower elevation land for full time living where food can be grown more easily." (Skousen, 2013).

Regional Considerations

There are many factors to take into consideration when searching for that ideal country property. Some of the main issues might be garden growing seasons, weather, potential natural dangers, terrain of the property, local economy, governmental regulations, and military establishments in the region.

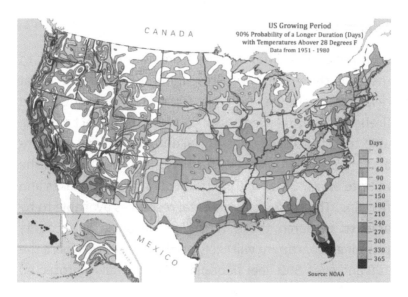

Gardening Growing Seasons Map source: NOAA

Weather Considerations

One major reason to relocate to country property is the ability to raise one's own provisions. Gardening potential should be of prime importance when considering where to live. Some regions have seasonal extremes such as very cold winters and very hot summers. Other regions that have distinct seasons may be more temperate, with less extreme seasonal temperature swings. Of course, if a person lives close to the equator it might be possible to grow produce year-round. But most people live farther from the equator, therefore, need to contemplate each of the seasonal impacts. Another item to consider is how much irrigation the garden will need to be in a particular climate and season. The availability of water is likely the most important requirement for a survival property location.

Natural Dangers

Each region has different risks from nature. One needs to research the risk of wildfires. If there was a fire, what response might be available from first responders and firefighters in that area? Also, consider the impact of being able to get insurance against wildfires. This may be more and more of a problem the further one moves out into the remote areas. Other natural risks could be earthquakes and flooding. There are governmental resources available to be able to research these risks. For instance, the county planning department will likely be able to tell you where the 100 and even 500-year floodplains are as well as protected wetlands.

Property Terrain

Sunshine availability is critical to gardening and solar power generation. It is vitally important to find a property that has adequate exposure to the sun throughout the year. I have heard of people looking to move into the country who have visited a property in the summer and bought the land without doing adequate due diligence. They found they did not have enough direct sunlight during the day because they were on the shaded side of a hill. Plus, in the winter, it not only hampered solar efforts, but they found that the winter snow did not melt off, making driveway cleaning more complicated. In the northern hemisphere, the property should have southern exposure to the sun. The ideal would be for the gardening space to have a slight downhill slant to the south, increasing the sun exposure in the winter months when the sun's arch is closer to the horizon. Finding a beautiful view up of high ground might vastly increase the cost of developing the property.

Microclimates

One might assume that higher elevations would be colder because there might be snow on the surrounding mountains and warmer temperatures in the valley. While that is true in a broader sense, some microclimates should be understood when looking at a region for country property. On a single 40-acre property there might be pockets of colder air due to the terrain of the land. Hot air rises, and cold air drifts to a low-lying area. Consequently, property on the edge of a lake may not be ideal for gardening compared to further up from the lake. The same is true even without a body of water. Some gardens are part-way up a hill and those in the valley will have frost earlier in the fall and later in the spring. These things are worth careful consideration when planning for a garden to have the longest growing season possible.

County and State Regulations

When considering a particular property, research any applicable county and state regulations as well as covenants that might be attached to the property. Covenants may be good, insuring against negative elements such as a neighbor having junk or a mean dog. On the other hand, most people prefer no covenants, leaving the owner freedom to develop their land and live on it how they wish. Government limitations might include whether you can have free use of your well water or surface water such as a creek. If you have a creek or spring with enough drop in elevation to give you the option to take advantage of that to generate electricity, can you? These kinds of things are worth taking into consideration when looking at property locations.

Adjacent Open Spaces

To ensure privacy now and into the future, it might be good to find a property that backs up against wilderness in the form of forestry or government land. Without this, it could be that in the future there could be a housing development or industrial complex in your backyard. Another item to consider about the adjacent property is if the property is next to farmland. Commercial crops may be using modern methods such as spraying Roundup before planting with GMO seeds. There have been instances where homeowners were unable to be successful at gardening while living next to a farm field because the spraying rendered their property unproductive. Also remember, if you don't own it, you can't control it. So, keep in mind that the neighboring properties may not always stay the way you see them. For instance, you might enjoy the privacy afforded by being surrounded by timberland, but a few years down the road everything around you could get logged! What a change that would be. Fortunately, over time the trees would grow back, regaining your privacy once again.

Military Risks

Our last regional consideration when looking for an area to find land is the risks that might be within the proximity of military establishments. During wartime, it is likely that a nuclear target could be a military base. Even remote places like Montana and North Dakota have a surprising number of potential targets due to hidden missile silos. See the book *Strategic Relocation* for maps to show areas with potential military targets.

Beautiful Country Property image used with permission from David Battler

Ideal Country Wish List

It is important to understand that there is no perfect property. One will never find a parcel of land that does not have some negative factors. The goal here is to find the one best suited for you, all things considered. My suggestion is to start by narrowing the search from a large then smaller region of the country based on your personal and family needs. Factors that may play into this narrowing process might include employment opportunities and proximity to extended family members. Included in the Appendix is a sample wish list for regions, properties, and houses.

Combining the Needs of All Stakeholders

It is helpful for each person in the family to make their wish list for what they are looking for in a new country home. Then have each person rearrange their list to be in priority order, with the most important on the top of the list. Now, compare the individual lists of each person involved in the decision process. Attempt to find a compromise to negotiate one combined list in priority order. Remember not everything on the list is likely to be available at any property, but this process will help to ensure that all important criteria have been thought through when continuing the land search process.

Remote Employment

If you are fortunate enough to be able to work remotely, this would be ideal, affording you the option to live almost anywhere. Most likely, working remotely would require the availability of dependable Internet access. This could be in the form of DSL, cable, or fiber access to the property. In more remote cases, satellite access to the Internet could be a viable option. Be sure to look into each of these, including initial setup costs and monthly fees before purchasing the property. Another communication portal to consider is whether there is cell service available at the property. Sometimes an affordable Internet option could be via the cell service company. If you are planning on working remotely, it would be favorable to have a backup plan if remote work is no longer an option.

Local Employment

Check out if there are employment opportunities in that area that fit your experience and skill set. If not, are you willing to learn a new trade to find employment in this new area? Consider the wages offered for work in that area and compare the cost of living needed for you to be able to live in that location. Remember to factor in the costs of annual land taxes.

Other Factors

For each family, there will be different needs and criteria on those wish lists. It might be proximity to family, especially with aging parents. They may wish to be close to their growing families, especially grandchildren. Another factor might be schooling for the children. If you have or plan to have children, are you going to homeschool or wish to live near enough for the option of a good public or Christian school? These kinds of considerations are examples of the many varied things that you may have unique to your own family's needs when searching for the ideal country property.

Pray for God's Leading

The Bible promises, "And we know that all things work together for good to those who love God, to those who are the called according to *His* purpose." Romans 8:28. (NKJV, 2020). Therefore, if we are moving to the country because God has called us to do that, then we need to depend on Him to help us find the very property He has in mind for us.

References

Skousen, J. M. (2013). *Strategic Relocation: North American Guide to Safe Places,* (3rd ed., p. 118). Printing Resource

The New King James Version, 2020, Romans 8:28.

Additional Video and Podcast Resources

Video Supplement to Chapter 32
www.preparingforthetimeoftrouble.com - Part 464
"What to Look for in Country Property"

www.preparingforthetimeoftrouble.com – Part 334
"Country Living Testimony – Thompson Falls, Montana"

Chapter 33: How to Find Good Country Property

Most people who are thinking about moving out of the city into the country are told about things to look for when buying. I have attended many seminars on moving to the country and most of the time is spent talking about looking for something to buy. This is fine if you are able to purchase, but some are unable and can rent a country property.

What About Me?

Most of the time when I have done a presentation on moving to the country, someone during the question-and-answer period says, "But what about me in my situation?" These scenarios can include a young family with little or no money to purchase. It might be an old widow who is no longer physically able to do the heavy lifting of farm life.

God Can Find a Way

I believe if God places a burden on your heart to move into the country, He can find a way that will work for you. An example might be two parties teaming up, such as the young couple with not enough money and the elderly widow. The young couple might be physically fit and willing to work, while the older woman may own her country property but need some help. That is something to pray for God's leading to find the best situation in the country.

Finding Good Country Property

The focus of this chapter, though, is to deal with how to find good country property. While this will mostly suit someone who wants to purchase, some of the principles may also be applicable to others, such as a family able to rent a country place. In the previous chapter, we looked at narrowing the search to a local area. In this chapter, we will talk about various tools and methods that can be helpful in doing the search for that special piece of property.

Property For Sale image source: Library of Congress

Renting First

First, even if you are planning to buy, there might be merit in renting first if you are new to the area. This will allow you to learn about idiosyncrasies of that area such as microclimates. For instance, someone living on a hill will have a different frequency of frost than someone living in the valley. I used to think that living higher up would equate with colder weather. Our experience with country properties has proven just the opposite! So, living for a period of time in the area would possibly allow you to interact with locals and find out these kinds of important things.

Start with Open Listings

Thinking back on one of our past searches for country property, I started with real estate listings. The Internet allows you to search for properties for sale from the convenience of your house, even if you live hundreds of miles away. Several real estate websites include a map with icons showing the listings, and by clicking on the icon, you can get more details. This may lead you to that perfect property, or at least help you become educated as to market values and availability. Some sites list properties for sale by owner such as https://fsbo.com/, or general listing sites with categories for real estate for sale by owner such as www.craigslist.com.

Visit the Locations

Once you have exhausted the posted online listings, it's time to travel to the locations. Using the listings of interest, you can start by looking at the listed properties in person. Many times, what shows in the pictures in a listing is more glamorous than reality once you see things in person. For instance, I know of a person who had a very beautiful country property for sale but when you drove to see it, one had to pass a very trashy neighbor's place on the way.

Firsthand Look

Going to see the listings in person also gives you a firsthand look at the general area. Is this area beautiful and peaceful? Are the properties in the area well-maintained? Are there some negative elements in the area such as unmaintained shared roads? Are the high-tension powerlines on the property? Is there a train track nearby?

Beyond Listed Properties

Now that you have narrowed your search to finding small areas you particularly like, don't be limited by listed properties for sale. I have heard of a couple who looked at a property for sale but ended up buying the adjacent parcel that was not listed for sale. They drove up the driveway and introduced themselves and the owners ended up selling to the couple.

County Resources

Some free tools can be used as you look at parcels available in the country. Most counties have options online, but if not, they are available in person at the county planning office. Online county records will tell you who owns the property and whether they live there. If you walked up to a house you liked and asked if they wanted to sell, they might say no, and you might not realize they are not the owners. The county parcel information will tell who the owner is, where the owner lives, how much they paid for it and when, what the taxes are, etc. The details in the legal description might also unearth critical information like easements.

Homeowner Association

Research to see if the property has any Homeowner Association (HOA) attached to the land. Some people prefer the protection that HOAs offer, limiting negative elements of neighbors, while many prefer to have no HOAs, affording complete freedom. The county parcel information would also include a photo of the house, how many acres the property is, and a map of the land. This map is helpful because you can often see the neighboring parcels on the map.

Google Maps and Google Earth

Google Maps is a very useful tool to use on your smartphone as you drive to the properties. It not only can direct you to the property but allows you to see an overhead view of the area with optional views of the default as well as satellite and terrain views. This will help you see if the land is steep or flat. Google Earth is even more sophisticated with the ability to accurately see the height of the highest point on the property as compared to the lowest. It can show you the longitude and latitude as well as a 3D view option. Zooming back will allow you to see what is over the hill that you might not be aware of on a physical visit.

Wetlands and Floodplains

One more important aspect to research in county records is does the property include areas of designated wetlands. These are part of the land that cannot be built on. Also, check with the county about flood plains. They should have a map with 100-year floodplain designations and possibly 500-year floodplain projections.

Well Logs

Another property feature that the county would have a record of is any wells on the property. A well log is an official document stating how deep the well is and the possible gallons per minute. If you are serious about purchasing a property with or without a well, it would be good to introduce yourself to your immediate neighbor and ask about their water supply. Is it good water? Do they have to treat it? How deep is their well? Do they run out seasonally? The quality of the neighbor's water would likely be a good indicator of water available on your property.

Available Utilities

When on-site, investigate whether there is a well, a septic system, electricity, phone, cell service, and Internet access. Carefully check the road access. Does the property border the county road or not? If not, is the road shared with neighbors? Who maintains it? A county road would be cleared of snow while a private road may not.

Before You Sign

An article by James Fitzgerald says, "Before signing on any dotted lines, you'll need to check on zoning and any potential restrictions on the land you're thinking about buying. To start, be aware of the zoning rules for the land. All land is zoned for a specific use: residential, commercial, and agricultural. With each classification there are different sets of rules established by zoning commissions for individual counties or cities. This will determine what you are and aren't allowed to build on the land." (Fitzgerald, 2023).

No Perfect Place

Remember, there is no perfect place. You will likely not ever find everything you want on your wish list. When you do find the best property, you can decide whether to buy it, but make sure to use a title office to process the transaction. Even if the owner is willing to hold a contract, allowing you to make payments to them, have a title office process the deal to ensure a safe final transaction and avoid unforeseen problems.

Personal Experience

In our own family's experience, we have found that praying to God will lead us to the right property and make the best decision, giving us peace of mind and no regrets. We have seen that approach results in many miraculous turns of events in the process of finding that ideal place in the country.

References

Fitzgerald, J. (2023, September 29). *How to buy land: A step-by-step guide*. Family Handyman. https://www.familyhandyman.com/article/how-to-buy-land/

Additional Video and Podcast Resources

Video Supplement to Chapter 33
www.preparingforthetimeoftrouble.com - Part 465
"How to Find Good Country Property"

www.preparingforthetimeoftrouble.com - Part 21
"What to Look for in Country Property"

www.preparingforthetimeoftrouble.com – Part 23
"How to Find Good Country Property"

www.preparingforthetimeoftrouble.com – Part 327
"Finding Country Property"

Chapter 33: How to Find Good Country Property

Chapter 34: Dangers of Household Mold

There was a time when I was asked by a friend to help them look at country property that they were considering purchasing. It had many positive features that made this place quite appealing. They had looked at this particular parcel more than once and wanted me to evaluate as they came close to making a final decision.

Looking at Country Property

We met the realty agent at the property to have a walk-through. It had a nicely remodeled, large home plus a cute outbuilding that the owners used as a game room including an outdoor fireside picnic area. The parcel of land would accommodate plenty of room for a large garden and orchard.

Black Mold

There had already been a professional house inspection, revealing some minor issues and one larger concern. As we toured the house, we were taken to the upper level of the house to find a drop-down ladder leading to the large attic space. The attic had a floor and lots of headroom. Unfortunately, the entire ceiling was covered with a splattering of black mold. This appeared to have happened due to not having proper attic ventilation.

Deal Killer

Typically, an attic has vents along the bottom and top of the attic spaces allowing convection to naturally allow for airflow. This was not done, therefore the mold had formed. In an attempt to remedy the situation, the owner had installed fans that ran 24/7. Even though it appeared that some remediation efforts might remove the mold, ultimately my friends decided to not purchase the home.

Professional Home Inspection

When looking for your country home, it is important to have a professional home inspection done to unearth any areas of concern that a casual visit might not reveal. This home needed some repairs done under the house to improve the insulation as well as some improvements to the furnace room. Each of these issues could have easily been solved by hiring a professional, and those costs could have been used as a bargaining wedge in the process of finalizing an offer.

But mold is an entirely different problem. This is because it can result in very dangerous health risks.

Leaky Roof

Another building I was involved with, it was discovered that the roofing contractor had not properly installed the roof. Consequently, black mold had formed on two different walls in the building. Interestingly, mold does not affect some people noticeably, while others can have long-term, life-altering problems.

Symptoms

The New York Department of Health says, "Although symptoms can vary, the most common symptoms seen in people exposed to mold indoors include: nasal and sinus congestion, eye irritation, such as itchy, red, watery eyes, wheezing and difficulty breathing, cough, throat irritation, skin irritation, such as a rash, [and] headache." (NYDOH, 2022).

Serious Health Threat

BioTerra Environmental Solutions, a mold remediation company, states "Because toxic mold exposure can be a serious health threat, it's important that you get professional help if you think you might have dangerous mold in your home. The first step is to have your home professionally tested for mold. This should involve a thorough inspection for any water damage or mold growth found on materials in your home, as well as an air quality test to check for airborne spores... Next, samples will be sent to an environmental testing laboratory to determine if there are harmful species of mold in your home. If needed, you can then call in a mold remediation company to remove the toxic mold in your home and get to the bottom of any remaining sources of water damage. Once the mold has been remediated, a clearance air test can be performed to ensure that the mold levels in your home are safe." (BioTerra, 2019).

Types of Household Mold

According to BioTerra, there are six types of household mold: Stachybotrys, Chaetomium, Aspergillus, Penicillium, Fusarium, and Alternaria.

Black mold is the common name for Stachybotrys. Typically, it is found in damp areas in the house. This is one of the most dangerous forms of household mold and can be particularly injurious to young children because their lungs are still under development.

Water damage to areas in a house often will result in Chaetomium. These are found in dark damp areas such as drywall and baseboards. These spores can cause autoimmune diseases and neurological damage.

Aspergillus spores are common in the air and generally are harmless except for those with a compromised immune system. It can also create lung infections, allergic reactions, and an infection known as aspergillosis.

Penicillium is also found in common air, but when trapped in a house can cause respiratory issues.

Fusarium is found in plant debris and soil but can sometimes make its way under carpets or HVAC systems in houses. Sometimes eye infections can result.

Alternaria is a well-known mold that can cause allergies and is most prevalent in humid areas during spring and summer seasons. It can be found in homes on cardboard and electrical cables. (BioTerra, 2019).

Exposed Black Mold image used with permission from Jim Gurtner

House Rental Mold

One of my family friends had an encounter with household mold. They were renting a home not realizing it had mold. After becoming sick, they found that mold was creating serious health problems. Ultimately, they were forced to throw away almost all their household belongings including paintings her mother had made for them. Fortunately, the mother was kind enough to recreate some of the paintings.

Basement Mold

Another acquaintance of mine told of his family storing some of their household belongings in their mother's basement as they were transitioning to a country home. As a result of the mold in the mother's basement, one of the family members got terribly sick. They had to throw away everything stored in the basement. To make matters worse, when they bought their country home, they discovered black mold again to be an issue. With the family member already sick from mold, they were forced to purchase a brand-new mobile home to live in while they embarked on a full-scale mold remediation of the house. This major undertaking was even so extreme that they had to even remove the furnace heat ducts to eliminate every remaining mold residue. Despite all these expenses and mitigation efforts, they chose to move. You can hear the whole story directly from the homeowner by watching the three videos linked below.

Mold Testing Before Buying

The final takeaway from this chapter is when a person is looking for a country property, it is very important to have a thorough house inspection, including a mold test, prior to final purchasing. My suggestion would be to make that a contingency of a purchase offer. Any needed remediation efforts should be done by a professional company at the expense of the owner prior to the closing. A person's health is too important to overlook this important aspect of looking for that ideal country property.

References

NYDOH. Mold and Your Home: What You Need to Know. (2022, November). https://www.health.ny.gov/publications/7287/

Bioterra. (2019). *6 types of harmful mold that may be lurking in your home*. Bioterra Solutions. https://bioterrasolutions.com/blog/6-types-of-harmful-mold/

Additional Video and Podcast Resources

www.preparingforthetimeoftrouble.com – Part 195 "Mold in Your Country Home and Your Health"

www.preparingforthetimeoftrouble.com – Part 196 "Country Home Mold Testing"

www.preparingforthetimeoftrouble.com – Part 197 "Country Home Mold Remediation"

Chapter 35: Passive Solar Architectural Design

.

Most of the time, people who are moving from the city to the country will be able to find a functioning homestead with much of the buildings and infrastructure already in place. In most cases, this would be ideal for several reasons. One, you know up front exactly how much it will cost as compared to developing the property and building a house. Secondly, it saves lots of complications because you can just move in and begin enjoying the country life without all the challenges of construction.

Building a House

If you decide to build a house on the property, it would be a good idea to seriously consider the design of the house to capitalize on the warmth the sun can provide. Most homes are not planned with the sun in mind. I knew someone who bought undeveloped land and proceeded to use a "cookie-cutter" house plan out of a magazine. The problem is the house plan was not designed for that piece of property. In their case, the front door was on the side of the house and was not even visible from the driveway or parking area. The visitor would be confused and possibly would use the back door instead. This type of poor planning often happened in old farm properties, resulting in the front door rarely, if ever being used.

House Design

Let's consider how to take advantage of the sun when looking for or drawing a house plan. We discussed earlier in this book how the sun needs to be taken into consideration to take advantage of solar gain. This is important for generating electricity with solar panels as well as the need for as much sun as possible for the garden. The house design we are talking about is called passive solar.

House Heating

Houses can be heated by a variety of methods, one of which is a wood stove, which we discussed in an earlier chapter. By incorporating passive solar design into the house plans, a person can use the sun to help heat the house in the winter and avoid the heat in the summer.

How Passive Solar Design Works

The government agency Energy Saver explains, "A passive solar home collects heat as the sun shines through south-facing windows and retains it in materials that store heat, known as thermal mass. The share of the home's heating load that the passive solar design can meet is called the passive solar fraction and depends on the area of glazing and the amount of thermal mass. The ideal ratio of thermal mass to glazing varies by climate. Well-designed passive solar homes also provide daylight all year and comfort during the cooling season through the use of nighttime ventilation." (Energy Saver, 2023).

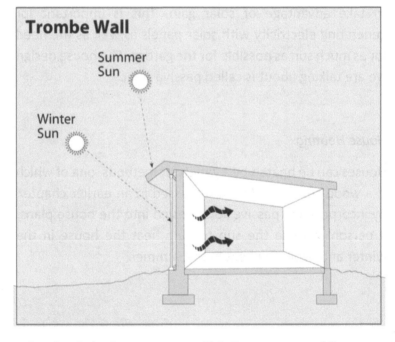

Passive Solar image source: U.S. Department of Energy

Key Elements

Energy Saver also suggests the key elements of good passive solar house design. The windows on the south side of the house need to face 30 degrees of true south during the colder months and be shaded during the summer months by roof overhangs, or vegetation such as grape leaves. Next thermal mass needs to be considered which is some dense material to absorb the heat of the sun during the winter days. These can be concrete, stone, brick, or tile. It could even be a rockery such as in a water feature.

Distribution by Convection

Distribution of the heat or cooling can be done by convection, using mother nature to move the air through the house, or with a mechanical method such as fans. The passive method works by using convection. Since hot air rises, there can be airflow designed into the house plan including how the opening windows are arranged. Radiation is the process of heat escaping from a hotter object to the nearby cooler air. So, if the design incorporates some mass that absorbs and stores the heat from the sun, then later it will radiate that heat into the air. Properly designed, this method can help absorb, store, and release heat from the sun long after the sun is down. The National Renewable Energy Laboratory explains that in the purest sense, "Passive solar technologies convert sunlight into usable heat and cause air movement for ventilating to heat and cool living spaces without active mechanical or electrical devices." (NREL, 2023).

Increasing Efficiency

There are several important ways to increase the efficiency of these passive solar design efforts. First, make sure the home has enough insulation or all those efforts might be ineffective. Next, be sure the windows are of a high insulation value. Old houses with single-pane windows are very inefficient and should not be used. Double pane windows are in most homes these days, and if far north, in very cold climates, some houses even have triple pane glass designs.

Sunrooms

An optional way to capitalize on the sun when needed would be to incorporate a sunroom. This added space on the house would be like an attached greenhouse or solarium which will generate a great deal of sun heat because the roof and south-facing wall would be mostly glass. In the summer months, this room could be ventilated and closed off from the rest of the house. The nice thing about a sunroom is that it can be used as a comfortable, additional living space which can be even used on overcast summer days or sunny winter days. The following picture shows how a covered porch can be enclosed to create a sunroom.

Sunroom image source: Pixabay

Whether you are planning a design for a house to build on your country property or if you have or plan to purchase an already existing home in the country, it is worth some serious thought about ways that you can take advantage of the additional heat that the sun can afford you.

References

Energy Saver. (2023). *Passive Solar Homes*. Energy.gov. https://www.energy.gov/energysaver/passive-solar-homes

NREL. (2023). *Passive Solar Technology Basics*. https://www.nrel.gov/research/re-passive-solar.html

Chapter 36: Balancing Physical and Spiritual Preparation

Christians often have a special interest in what the Bible prophecies foretell about the future. Daniel 12 tells us that there will be a Time of Trouble such as never has been or ever will be again. The prophecies in the book of Revelation tell of a time when those who are faithful to God will not be allowed to buy or sell because they will not accept the mark of the beast.

Being Self-Sustaining

Forward-thinking believers in these prophecies often consider ways to become self-sustaining, weaning off the need to depend on the systems of the world to survive. God promises that He will take care of those who are faithful, but also expects us to do our part. God did not give us a glimpse into the future through prophecy for us to be afraid, but for us to be prepared to stand in those troublesome times to come.

Fear Not

Jesus said, "Let not your heart be troubled, neither let it be afraid... And now I have told you before it comes, that when it does come to pass, you may believe." (John 14:27, 29 NKJV). The Bible also says, "For God has not given us a spirit of fear, but of power and of love and of a sound mind." (2 Timothy 1:7 NKJV).

Atomic Bomb Blast image source: Library of Congress

Preparations Falling Short

We can see then that God does not want us to worry or fret about the troublesome times we may face ahead, whether man-made or prophetically predicted. Even with our best physical preparations, we likely would fall short of being completely self-sustaining during difficult times ahead. For instance, no matter how big a garden you might have, it is likely that there would not be enough for your family to be able to share with others.

Earthly Treasures

Jesus further counseled us, "Do not lay up for yourselves treasures on earth, where moth and rust destroy and where thieves break in and steal; but lay up for yourselves treasures in heaven, where neither moth nor rust destroys and where thieves do not break in and steal. For where your treasure is, there your heart will be also." (Matthew 6:19-21 NKJV). Many doomsday preppers appear to be laying up treasures of provisions out of fear, to depend on themselves for troubled times coming, but not depending on God to see them through. As we will discuss further in the next chapter, there can be a stark contrast between the worldly, doomsday prepper and the Christian who is preparing physically as well as spiritually.

Gideon's Efforts

A good Bible story to understand the balance is found in what happened to Gideon in fighting the Midianites. Gideon started out with a mass army of 10,000 Israelite soldiers, but God whittled them down to 300, so their promised victory over their enemies would not be credited to them, but to God's delivering them. (Judges 7 NKJV). Even though God promised to Gideon that they would be victorious in the battle, they marched all night and put out every effort as though the success of the battle weighed solely on their efforts. God blessed their faith in Him and their honest efforts to give them victory. Using an army of 300, God miraculously overcame an enemy of 120,000 soldiers! The moral of this story seems to be that God promises to give us victory if we do our part and follow His directions. He does not expect us to assume miracles will happen without any effort on our part.

Being Good Stewarts

We need to be good stewards of what blessings God has given to us. Jesus warned us not to lay up worldly treasures but to have our focus on heavenly things. If we are preparing for troubled times selfishly then God cannot bless our efforts. We likely will not be willing to stand faithful when the real test comes of whether to accept the mark of the beast or not.

Mark of the Beast Test on Forehead and on Right Hand

When the Bible describes the mark of the beast test, there will only be two classes of people: those who accept the mark and those who do not. More specifically, the Bible describes those who accept the mark as having it on their forehead *or* on their right hand. (Revelation 13:16 NKJV). Those who are faithful are described as only having God's seal on their forehead. (Revelation 7:3 NKJV).

Seal of God on Forehead

So why would the seal of God and the mark of the beast be on the person's forehead, but the mark of the beast could optionally be on the right hand? Seems logical that having this designation as being on the forehead would indicate that the person believes either God or the devil. On the other hand, the devil's mark of the beast could optionally be on the right hand. Why?

Outside Pressures

Let's consider what happened during COVID-19 and the pressures to take the vaccine. There were entire areas of employment such as medical workers, police, and teachers that, in many states, were required to get vaccinated or lose their jobs. Those who were convicted of not taking the vaccine were willing to lose their jobs to live up to their beliefs. This would be symbolic of the forehead.

Symbolism

On the other side of these employment pressures, some chose to get vaccinated. Some did it because they fully had faith in the efficacy of the vaccine, symbolized by the forehead. Others did not want to take the vaccine and believed they should not but succumbed to the pressure because they wanted to keep their job, symbolized by the right hand.

Mark of the Beast Pressure

If this comparison of the mark of the beast and vaccine mandates is valid, it could help us understand the mark of the beast pressures. The requirement of the mark of the beast could result in people accepting the mark because they are fully convinced, or those who are not persuaded just give in to the pressure. On the other hand, those who choose not to take the mark of the beast will only make that choice because of personal conviction, not out of convenience.

Finding Balance

Now when we think back on our original issue of trying to find balance between making physical preparation and being spiritually prepared, of course being spiritually solid is the most important. Our main focus should not be about being prepared for difficult times. Rather we should be focused on being connected with God in such a way that we cannot be moved from trusting in God in all things. We can learn a lesson from the children of Israel in the wilderness. Their clothes and shoes did not even wear out, and God provided manna and water for them each day. God can be trusted to fill in the gaps where our preparations fall short.

Two Ditches of Extremes

In comparison to a road with a ditch on each side, we need to avoid falling into either ditch of extremes. One danger would only be focusing on our own efforts to prepare. The other risk would be doing nothing, expecting God to take care of us without any effort on our part. So, as we consider various ways to be sustainably prepared and live a self-sufficient country lifestyle, let's keep our focus where it ultimately belongs, on not being fearful but trusting in God for all things.

References

The New King James Version, 2020, John 14:27, 29.

The New King James Version, 2020, 2 Timothy 1:7.

The New King James Version, 2020, Matthew 6:19-21.

The New King James Version, 2020, Judges 7.

The New King James Version, 2020, Revelation 13:16.

The New King James Version, 2020, Revelation 7:3.

Additional Video and Podcast Resources

Video Supplement to Chapter 36
www.preparingforthetimeoftrouble.com - Part 463
"Balancing Physical and Spiritual Preparation"

www.preparingforthetimeoftrouble.com – Part 361
"Spiritual Preparation for Country Living"

Chapter 37: Christian Preppers vs. Doomsday Preppers

The Bible foretells a time when those who would not succumb to accepting the mark of the beast will not be able to buy or sell. Those who yield to the pressure of the beast will have a mark on their forehead or in their hand. Those Christians who stay faithful to God will not accept the mark but be sealed in their foreheads.

The Revelation of Jesus

Long after Jesus had died and returned to heaven, his remaining disciples suffered persecution and death while being faithful to Him. John, at an old age, was exiled to the prison island of Patmos. But while there, Jesus came to him, encouraging him, and revealing to him a panoramic view of what would happen in the future.

A Preview of the Future Troublous Times

Besides encouraging John with Jesus's visit in person at that death camp island, He revealed to John the times of trouble that would happen just before His return. The devil would steadily increase his attack on those faithful saints as time got closer to the second coming.

The Mark of the Beast and 666

The Bible in Revelation 13:16-18 prophesies, "He causes all, both small and great, rich and poor, free and slave, to receive a mark on their right hand or on their foreheads, and that no one may buy or sell except one who has the mark or the name of the beast, or the number of his name. Here is wisdom. Let him who has understanding calculate the number of the beast, for it is the number of a man: His number *is* 666." (NKJV, 2020).

The Time of Trouble

Hundreds of years earlier, the prophet Daniel had a similar experience as John did with his encounter with Jesus. Daniel was told by Jesus that there would be a time of tribulation like had never been or ever would be again. "At that time Michael shall stand up, the great prince who stands *watch* over the sons of your people; And there shall be a Time of Trouble, such as never was since there was a nation, *Even* to that time. And at that time your people shall be delivered, everyone who is found written in the book. And many of those who sleep in the dust of the earth shall awake, Some to everlasting life, some to shame *and* everlasting contempt." Daniel 12:1, 2 (NKJV, 2020).

The Promise of Jesus's Return

At the return of Jesus, those faithful to Him will be taken back to heaven with Him and eventually live forever in a newly transformed earthly home. Jesus promises us, "In My Father's house are many mansions; if *it were* not *so,* I would have told you. I go to prepare a place for you. And if I go and prepare a place for you, I will come again and receive you to Myself; that where I am, *there* you may be also." John 14:2, 3 (NKJV, 2020).

The Christian Viewpoint

Christians view things completely different than those of the world. We don't need to have a spirit of fear. "For God has not given us a spirit of fear, but of power and of love and of a sound mind." 2 Timothy 1:7 (NKJV, 2020). We can have peace even during troubling times. "Be anxious for nothing, but in everything by prayer and supplication, with thanksgiving, let your requests be made known to God; and the peace of God, which surpasses all understanding, will guard your hearts and minds through Christ Jesus." Philippians 4:6, 7 (NKJV, 2020).

The Christian Prepper

The book *Last Day Events* has an admonition to prepare, "Again and again the Lord has instructed that our people are to take their families away from the cities, into the country, where they can raise their own provisions, for in the future the problem of buying and selling will be a very serious one." (White, 1992). Here we see a reason to prepare; to be self-sustaining when the time comes when you cannot buy or sell if you do not accept the mark of the beast. So, while we have reason as Christians to do some preparing for the troublous times prophesied, we do not need to be fearful or worried. God will bless your efforts to do what he asks. "The storm is coming, relentless in its fury. Are we prepared to meet it?" (White, 1976). "I see the necessity of making haste to get all things ready for the crisis." (White, 1946).

Being Prepared

We have seen, in this book, different ways to prepare to be "off-grid", and independent of the services and products that we acquire. Just like having a garden can help you provide food for your family during those hard times, we have other things we presently depend on that require money. These include electricity, water, heat, financial transactions, medical help, and information connectivity. By having a backup plan for each of these areas of need, we can position ourselves to be more self-sustaining in the event of a large-scale natural disaster, EMP, nuclear war, famine, or society-wide financial collapse. Possibly more important is being able to help others in need when they are not able to buy or sell. "A time is coming when knowing how to survive apart from civilization will be crucial." (Franklin, 2023). The Bible says, "Be thou prepared, and prepare for thyself, thou, and all thy company that are assembled unto thee, and be thou a guard unto them." Ezekiel 28:7 (KJV, 2020).

Doomsday Preppers

When our family realized that we needed to move out of the city and become more independent of the systems of the world, I began researching different methods of preparation. At that time there was an ongoing television series produced by National Geographic titled "Doomsday Preppers". Each program visited three different families that were prepping and rated each of them based on their preps. My goal was to learn what I could about what other people were doing to help us come up with a plan of our own.

Fears and Preps

Each scenario asked the participants what they were afraid of, for which they were preparing. There were a wide variety of responses they identified as their particular fears. Collectively these included: economic collapse, massive earthquakes, rising ocean levels, super tsunami, catastrophic weather, global pandemic, polar shift, sudden climate change, solar flares, super volcano, hyperinflation, catastrophic oil crisis, EMP detonation, power grid down, terrorist attack, nuclear accident or war, civil unrest, martial law, the apocalypse, and the end of the world. You can see there are many good reasons for people to be fearful.

Storing Food

In every scenario of a family preparation, there was always some form of collecting food. Most of the time this included food that was capable of long-term storage, up to 20 years. While there were other common preps that most families identified, one prep seemed to always be a common need - collecting guns. Some of these people had very large arsenals of weapons and ammunition.

Gas Mask image source: Pixabay

Survival of the Fittest

A common explanation about their plans for defending their home and preparations was that if someone came on their property wanting food, the response would be firm and decisive. "We have food for ourselves and if you attempt to take any of it, we will shoot to kill." This may seem a bit extreme to the viewer of the TV show. Unfortunately, during a real-world survival situation, one might be surprised how many people would have collected guns and ammunition for defense.

What Would You Do?

As I continued to gather information about how to prepare for future troubling times, whether natural, manmade, or prophetic end-time events, I wondered what I would do in those kinds of situations. Then we attended a seminar series by Jere Franklin, author of the book, *You Can Survive*. At the end of the seminar, there was an opportunity to ask questions. Someone asked, "Let's say that you have moved to the country and have a garden big enough to feed your family year-round. When you can't buy or sell, someone comes onto your property and asks for help with sharing some of your food. What would you do?" (Franklin, 2013).

You Can Survive Book Cover image used with permission
from Linda Franklin

New Concept

To be honest with you, I had been so consumed with thinking about preparing for my own family's needs and had not contemplated that scenario. After the question was raised, Jere Franklin answered without a moment's thought, "I would give them food". He explained that he believed that there are examples in the Bible of this generosity.

The Widow's Last Meal

Elijah had a death wish over his head and fled to the wilderness. He came across a widow and her young son. There was a famine in the land. Consequently, she was down to just enough flour and oil to be able to bake one last morsel of bread for the two of them, then they would die of starvation. Elijah asked her to share her food with him, which she un-selflessly did. She was blessed for her faith in God and generosity toward Elijah, by stretching the quantity of the oil and flour. As a result, the three of them were able to eat every meal for years until the famine ended.

Sharing

If we are generous with what God blesses us with, we will have more than we need for our family's needs! So, what can be learned from this perspective of God-fearing and generous Christians? What we see is an extreme difference between the motivation and perspective of a doomsday prepper and a preparing Christian.

Creation vs. Evolution

As I contemplated how these were opposed to each other, I wondered why. My conclusion is that it has to do with creation vs. evolution. You see, if a person does not believe in the Biblical creation, then they believe in survival of the fittest. Darwinism takes from the animal kingdom the understanding that to survive, you must be the predator. They believe the weight of responsibility for survival lies on oneself.

Depending on a Higher Power

The Christian, on the other hand, believes there is a higher power beyond themselves. All that we have are blessings from God. "All good gifts come from the Lord". James 1:17 (NKJV, 2020). After comparing the doomsday preppers with the Christians preparing for the future, I want to have backup plans for the things that we must pay for. That way, when we are faced with the choice of whether to accept the mark of the beast, we will stand firm, trusting in God. Those preparations that we may have been fortunate enough to have done in advance, will help our family to not only be able to take care of our needs but be a blessing to others, just like the widow did when sharing with Elijah. I believe that God will expand our previous efforts of preparing as we share with others when we cannot buy or sell.

References

NKJV. (2020). The New King James Version, 2020, Revelation 13:16-18.

NKJV. (2020). The New King James Version, 2020, Daniel 12:1.

NKJV. (2020). The New King James Version, 2020, John 14:2, 3.

NKJV. (2020). The New King James Version, 2020, Philippians 4:6, 7.

White, E. G. (1992). *Last Day Events*. pp. 99, 100, Pacific Press Publishing Association.

White, E. G. (1976). *Maranatha*. p. 108. Review and Herald Publishing Association.

White, E. G. (1946). *Country Living*. p. 21. Review and Herald Publishing Association.

Franklin. (2023). *You Can Survive*. https://youcansurvive.org/

NKJV. (2020). The New King James Version, 2020, Ezekiel 28:7.

Franklin. (2013). *You Can Survive*. https://youcansurvive.org/

Additional Video and Podcast Resources

Video Supplement to Chapter 37
www.preparingforthetimeoftrouble.com - Part 462
"Christian Preppers vs. Doomsday Preppers"

Chapter 38: Warning Those in the Cities

The prophet John was shown, in vision, what would happen to the cities of the earth in the end. "Now the great city was divided into three parts, and the cities of the nations fell. And great Babylon was remembered before God, to give her the cup of the wine of the fierceness of His wrath. Then every island fled away, and the mountains were not found. And great hail from heaven fell upon men, *each hailstone* about the weight of a talent. Men blasphemed God because of the plague of the hail since that plague was exceedingly great." Revelation 16:19-21 (NKJV, 2020).

Warnings About Living in the Cities

Over the past 100 years, since the migration to the cities during the Industrial Revolution, there have been many warnings about living in the cities. Some of the benefits of moving from the cities to live in the country include avoiding evil influences, benefits from nature, improving health, growing closer to God, and being able to grow a garden and be self-sustaining. The future will have very troubling times for those living in the cities.

The Cities Shaken

The book *Last Day Events* predicts, "The end is near and every city is to be turned upside down every way. There will be confusion in every city. Everything that can be shaken is to be shaken and we do not know what will come next. The judgments will be according to the wickedness of the people and the light of truth that they have had. O that God's people had a sense of the impending destruction of thousands of cities, now almost given to idolatry. The time is near when large cities will be swept away, and all should be warned of these coming judgments." Last Day Events, p. 111. (White, 1992).

San Francisco and Oakland

These warnings of God's coming judgments on the wicked cities are during the seven last plagues just before Jesus' Second Coming. These descriptions seem to encompass all of the large cities in the world, but there have been some cities called out by name as being listed for destruction by God. The book *Last Day Events* records a caution penned in 1903, "San Francisco and Oakland are becoming as Sodom and Gomorrah, and the Lord will visit them. Not far hence they will suffer under His judgments." Last Day Events, p. 114 (White, 1992).

1906 Earthquake and Fire

Just a few years later the following warning was given, "Out of the cities, is my message at this time. Be assured that the call is for our people to locate miles away from the large cities. One look at San Francisco as it is today would speak to your intelligent minds, showing you the necessity of getting out of the cities." Last Day Events, p. 95 (White, 1992). This was stated on May 10, 1906, which was about a month before the massive fire that resulted from an earthquake in San Francisco on April 16, 1906.

San Francisco Earthquake and Fire of 1906 image source: Library of Congress

Worst Natural Disaster

The National Archives reported that "On the morning of April 18, 1906, a massive earthquake shook San Francisco, California. Though the quake lasted less than a minute, its immediate impact was disastrous. The earthquake also ignited several fires around the city that burned for three days and destroyed nearly 500 city blocks. Despite a quick response from San Francisco's large military population, the city was devastated. The earthquake and fires killed an estimated 3,000 people and left half of the city's 400,000 residents homeless... The San Francisco earthquake is considered one of the worst natural disasters in U.S. history." (NARA, 2020). Was it pure coincidence that the warning to get out of San Francisco was barely a month prior to its destruction? Could it be that this is a wake-up call for later predictions as we read from the book of Revelation?

New York City

And what about New York City? "God has not executed His wrath without mercy. His hand is stretched out still. His message must be given in Greater New York. The people must be shown how it is possible for God, by a touch of His hand, to destroy the property they have gathered together against the last great day." Last Day Events, p. 112 (White, 1992). Is it possible that the dark day of 911 was a warning call for the cities?

September 11 Aftermath image source: Library of Congress

September 11 Attacks

The attacks on September 11, 2001, "killed nearly 3,000 people and injured more than 6,000 others in the worst attack against the homeland in our nation's history." (USDS, 2023). Again, is it possible that the dark day of 911 was a warning call for the cities?

Warning Those in the Cities

With the prophecy from the book of Revelation showing that the cities of the world will be destroyed, wouldn't Christians do well to attempt to warn those in the cities of the coming doom? How would you feel if you met someone after a similar devastation of their city much like we have seen happen to San Francisco and New York City? How would you feel if they said, "You knew this and never warned us?"

Warning of Doom

These are sobering things to consider. Of course, if you stood on a street corner with a sign warning of doom, today's modern people would walk by in disgust and assume you were just an alarmist. So, what is one to do? What approach should we take to heed the call to warn a lost world?

Lead by Example

The first thing would be to lead by example. We should move our families into the country, not only to get out of future harm's way but to live a happier, healthier, more abundant life closer to God's nature. We need to spend time in the Bible to learn more about what is coming and what God would have us do to help others.

Divine Appointments

It is important to pray for God to bring into our lives people whom we can touch with the saving truth. "For God so loved the world that He gave His only begotten Son, that whoever believes in Him should not perish but have everlasting life.

For God did not send His Son into the world to condemn the world, but that the world through Him might be saved." John 3:16 (NKJV, 2020).

References

White, E. G. (1992). *Last Day events.* Pacific Press Pub.
     Assn.

NARA. (2020). *San Francisco earthquake, 1906.* National
     Archives and Records Administration.
     https://www.archives.gov/legislative/features/sf

USDS. (2023). *22nd anniversary of the September 11, 2001
     attacks - united states department of state.* U.S.
     Department of State. https://www.state.gov/22nd-
     anniversary-of-the-september-11-2001-attacks/

Additional Video and Podcast Resources

www.preparingforthetimeoftrouble.com - Part 362
"Warning Against the Cities"

www.preparingforthetimeoftrouble.com – Part 3
"The Loud Cry and the Warning to the Cities"

www.preparingforthetimeoftrouble.com – Part 71
"Cities of the Nations Fell"

www.preparingforthetimeoftrouble.com – Part 81
"The Tenth of the City Fell"

Chapter 38: Warning Those in the Cities

Addendum: Property Wish List

There is no perfect country property, but the following is a list of things to think about when considering a particular parcel for sale. Look at each item and prioritize which ones are the most important for your family's needs.

LOCAL REGION CONSIDERATIONS	SUSTAINABILITY VALUE
Employment in the same career	Important
Employment in another career area	Important
State regulations about water use	Important
State regulations about homeschooling	Important
Proximity to power transmission lines	Negative
Proximity to noisy railroad	Negative

Property tax rate	Important
Regulations preventing use of creek (hydro)	Important
Weather patterns (rain, wind, etc.)	Important
Risk of wildfires	Important
Risk of landslides	Important

PROPERTY CONSIDERATIONS	SUSTAINABILITY VALUE
Location	Important
South-facing for solar and gardening	Important
Soil (gardening)	Important
Microclimates	Important
First and last frost dates	Helpful
Number of cold days	Helpful
Days without rain	Helpful
Firewood source on the property	Important
Access to county road (direct or easement)	Important
Road maintenance (snow removal, etc.)	Important
Wetlands	Negative
Floodplain	Negative
Distance from freeway	Important
Proximity to power transmission lines	Negative
Water source (well, spring)	Important

Water treatment (filters, UV, softener, etc.)	As needed
Electrical power	Important
Septic system (conventional)	Preferred
Engineered septic system (pressure or mound)	Not preferred
Cell service availability	Important
Internet availability	Important
Noise (traffic, industry, railroad)	Important
Neighbors	Important
Homeowners Association (HOA)	Negative
Zoning	Important
Covenants	Negative
Groundwater (creek, etc.)	Desirable
Water rights (creek, etc.)	Important
Rainwater collection restrictions	Negative
Mineral rights	Not critical
Privacy	Important

View	Nice but not necessary
Property size (five acres or more)	Important
Adjacent to wilderness (timberland, forest service, etc.)	Very nice but not critical
Nearby industry (mining, livestock, paper mill, etc.)	Negative
Fire district (is it in one?)	Important
Affordability	Important
Is this a good investment? (see assessed value)	Important

HOUSE CONSIDERATIONS	SUSTAINABILITY VALUE
When built	Important
Overall condition	Important
Professional inspection (mold, rot, etc.)	Important
Source of heat	Important
Alternate source of heat (when away)	Important
House insulation	Important
Double-paned windows	Important
Fire-resistant roof (metal)	Ideal but not required
Fire-resistant siding (composite)	Ideal but not required
Existing alternative energy (solar, etc.)	Desirable
Wood stove	Important

About the Author

Donn Leiske is an international seminar presenter on the subjects of country living and preparedness for future troubled times. As a lifelong educator, Donn and his family have been practicing the country living lifestyle for most of their lives, attempting to avoid the dangers of the large urban centers and enjoy the beauty and solitude of nature while being self-sustaining. Donn is an author, produces videos on the "Preparing for the Time of Trouble" YouTube channel, hosts the website www.preparingforthetimeoftrouble.com and emails the End Time Updates.